PHILIP JODIDIO

NEW FORMS

ARCHITECTURE IN THE 1990S

TASCHEN

KÖLN LISBOA LONDON NEW YORK PARIS TOKYO

Cover
Frank O. Gehry
Guggenheim Museum
Bilbao, Spain, 1991–97
(see page 89)

Page 3
Philip Johnson
Gate House
New Canaan, Connecticut, 1995

Page 5
Enric Miralles
Unazuki Meditation Center
Toyama, Japan, 1991–93
(drawings)

About the author and editor:
Philip Jodidio was born in New Jersey
in 1954. He studied art history and
economics at Harvard, and has been
editor-in-chief of the French art
magazine *Connaissance des Arts* in Paris
since 1980. He has published numerous
studies on contemporary architecture.

© 2001 TASCHEN GmbH
Hohenzollernring 53, D-50672 Köln
www.taschen.com

Edited by Silvia Kinkel, Cologne
Co-edited by Christine Fellhauer, Cologne
Design and layout: Marion Hauff, Milan
Cover design: Catinka Keul, Cologne

Printed in Italy
ISBN 3-8228-1233-1

Contents

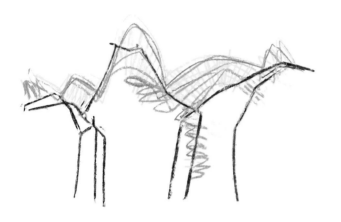

7   **INTRODUCTION**
New Geometries

51   **URBAN STRATEGIES**
Transport, Communications,
Tall Buildings and the Urban Nomad

81   **SPACE FOR ART**
A new Generation of Museums

109   **PLACES OF GATHERING**
Congress, Worship, Sport and Study

143   **ART AND ARCHITECTURE**
Breaking down the Barriers

179   **OUTLOOK**
Shapes for the Future

227   **BIOGRAPHIES**

234   **BIBLIOGRAPHY**

236   **INDEX**

237   **CREDITS**

INTRODUCTION

New Geometries

Philippe Starck
Le Baron Vert/Le Baron Rouge
Osaka, Japan, 1990
One of a series of unusually shaped buildings created by this French designer for Japan, the Baron Vert has a kind of monumentality, or a monolithic quality that seems to be inspired by his object designs. Although he sees himself as an architect as much as a designer, Starck has had difficulty completing built projects in France.

Setting the Scene: From Post-Modernism to Deconstructivism

For economic, technological and historical reasons the period between 1985 and 1995 will be remembered as one of fundamental change in art and architecture. The 1980s were of course a time of economic excess, when "Golden Boys" ruled the financial markets, and record prices were paid even for insignificant works of art. "Easy money" and uncritical demand went hand in hand to boost construction and to encourage a closer link between a certain consciousness of fashion, and artistic and architectural creativity. This was all to end for reasons linked to such events as the October 1987 collapse of the New York stock market, or the fall of the Berlin Wall in 1989. In a new climate of doubt and economic restrictions, architecture would be obliged to take new forms. The fact that this shift occurred just when the computer began to offer new design possibilities has demonstrably accentuated the emergence of a whole gamut of architectural solutions and shapes that could not have been imagined earlier.

Set loose from the rigorous constraints of rectilinear Modernist geometry as early as 1966, the date of Robert Venturi's seminal essay "Complexity and Contradiction in Architecture," many architects had searched throughout the 1970s for a valid equation between the demands of modern society and the siren-call of history. The resulting Post-Modernism, though largely superficial in its references to the past, did succeed in breaking down the intellectual barrier that existed between the contemporary and the pre-modern. Essentially a question of facades in its heyday, Post-Modernism led clearly to a more profound examination of the links that could be established with history. When Richard Meier, a leading figure of contemporary Modernist design, describes the Getty Center, his massive complex now under construction in Los Angeles, he says, "In my mind I keep returning to the Romans – to Hadrian's Villa, to Caprarola for their sequence of spaces, their thick-walled presence, their sense of order, the way in which building and landscape belong to each other." In this project, an architecture that could not be classified as Post-Modern, despite the use of an unusual cleft travertine cladding for the lower facades, is laid out in a complex pattern that certainly recalls Hadrian's Villa.

Although most criticism of architecture does not link it specifically to trends in the arts and to larger factors of the economy or even history, it seems obvious that, at the very least, intriguing coincidences do occur. It is almost always difficult to establish a one-to-one relationship between a given historical or economic event and a development in the arts, if only because the creative process is not oriented to such specific inspiration. Rather, a mood or a climate is established, and its influence may be so pervasive as to give rise to an esthetic response that is almost involuntary on the part of the creator. This is nothing other than the spirit of the times.

Though it might not be fruitful to attempt to establish any direct link, it is interesting to note that the October 1987 fall of the stock markets was followed in June 1988 by the "Deconstructivist Architecture" exhibition at the Museum of Modern

Art in New York. Uniting mostly unbuilt work by Frank O. Gehry, Daniel Libeskind, Rem Koolhaas, Peter Eisenman, Zaha Hadid, Bernard Tschumi and Coop Himmelblau, this show was directed by none other than Philip Johnson, co-author with Henry-Russell Hitchcock of the 1932 classic *The International Style*. This was of course the book that, in relation to another MoMA exhibition, defined the predominant discourse of architecture practically up until the time of Venturi. Deconstructivist architecture, esthetically identifiable by its fragmented forms, may indeed have more to do with the philosophy of Jacques Derrida than with the ills of Wall Street, but just as collapsing economic indicators called into doubt the certainties of the period, so architecture challenged its own underlying beliefs. As Mark Wigley, associate curator of the MoMA show, wrote: "The disquiet these buildings produce is not merely perceptual; it is not a personal response to the work, nor even a state of mind. What is being disturbed is a set of deeply entrenched cultural assumptions which underlie a certain view of architecture, assumptions about order, harmony, stability and unity."[1] In terms of the evolution of architectural thinking since the time of Post-Modernism in the 1970s, another argument put forward by Mark Wigley deserves to be pointed out. "...Deconstructivist architecture," he writes, "does not constitute an avant-garde. Rather it exposes the unfamiliar hidden within the traditional. It is the shock of the old."[2]

Pages 8/9
Richard Meier
Getty Center
Los Angeles, California, 1985–97
Located on a hilltop in Brentwood, mid-way between the Pacific and downtown Los Angeles, the Getty Center covers 87,800 m², excluding entrance and parking facilities, occupying 9.7 ha of the 44.5 ha site. An adjoining 243 ha owned by the Getty Trust preserves the natural quality of the area. Below, an aerial view shows the entire complex. To the right, the inner courtyard of the Museum.

The Magnificent Seven

It was no accident that the seven architects chosen for the Museum of Modern Art's "Deconstructivist Architecture" exhibition have remained amongst the most influential figures in international architecture. Although interest in Deconstructivism waned rather quickly, the original link between these figures was at best tenuous. They were quite simply some of the most original minds in the field, and their continued success is more a tribute to their personal inventiveness than it is to the dominance of a group.

Born in Toronto in 1929, but long a resident of southern California, Frank O. Gehry, for one, is a craftsman of architectural forms distinguished by his close connection to the art world. In his 1989 acceptance speech for the coveted Pritzker Prize, he said: "My artist friends, like Jasper Johns, Bob Rauschenberg, Ed Kienholz and Claes Oldenburg, were working with very inexpensive materials – broken wood and paper – and they were making beauty. These were not superficial details, they were direct, and raised the question in my mind of what beauty was. I chose to use the craft available, and to work with craftsmen and make a virtue out of their limitations. Painting had an immediacy that I craved for in architecture. I explored the process of new construction materials to try giving feeling and spirit to form. In trying to find the essence of my own expression, I fantasized that I was an artist standing before a white canvas deciding what the first move should be."[3] It will be argued here that one of the most important factors in emerging new forms is a renewed link between art and architecture. Frank O. Gehry has been an outstanding pioneer of a movement that is undoubtedly far more profound than ephemeral Desconstructivist theories. He has helped to return architecture to the place it long occupied as one of the major arts.

One of Frank O. Gehry's more successful buildings is his Vitra Design Museum in Weil am Rhein, Germany, just over the border from Basel, Switzerland. Its interior has been compared to Kurt Schwitter's Merzbau (Hanover), and Gehry himself has spoken of "frozen motion" in referring to this building. Neither these references, nor the twisted volumes of the exterior of this 1989 structure, immediately call to mind the superposed diagonals said to be typical of Deconstructivist architecture. The reason for this apparent paradox is quite simple. Gehry's exploration of new forms is as much a product of the study of contemporary art as it is related to Russian Constructivism or German Expressionism. Both of those movements of course attempted to integrate architecture and art into a single effort to create the new.

Another of MoMA's seven is Zaha Hadid, born in Baghdad in 1950. Having studied under Rem Koolhaas at the Architectural Association (AA) in London, she went on to be one of the more influential exponents of the new status of architects as artists. In fact from the first, which is to say her 1983 first prize entry for the Peak Club in Hong Kong, Zaha Hadid has been almost better known for her drawings, executed in a style that has been called "exploded isometric projection," than for her rare built work. Her 1993 Vitra Fire Station, on the same Weil am Rhein site as Gehry's Design Museum, is the proof that she is capable of converting her unusual vision of architecture for a fragmented, unstable society into concrete, steel and glass. It is both visually arresting and apparently quite functional despite a number of difficult-to-use sharp interior corners.

Hadid's teacher at the AA, the Dutch architect Rem Koolhaas, is one of the more flamboyant figures of his generation. Born in Rotterdam in 1944, he too has only recently had the opportunity to translate theoretical ruminations into rather spectacular built form with the Euralille complex in northern France, and in particular with the Grand Palais, an enormous exhibition hall and conference center. Rem Koolhaas first achieved public attention with the 1978 publication of his book *Delirious New York* in which he argued that America's most important contribution to urban design has been what he called "Manhattanism" – the congested high-rise cores of the largest cities. His theory is that that the glory of the city lies in the exceptional, the excessive, the extreme, in what he calls the "Culture of congestion." He proposes collaborating with, if not emulating, uncontrolled forces of develop-

Pages 10/11
Frank O. Gehry
Vitra International Furniture Manufacturing Facility and Museum
Weil am Rhein, Germany, 1986–89
The Vitra Design Museum serves mainly to exhibit the firm's large collection of chairs. Despite the apparent complexity of the structure, it functions well as a display facility, and is not plagued by unusable interior spaces. Sculptural in its volumes, Gehry's architecture here comes close to mostly unbuilt designs of the 1920s and 1930s, and goes beyond the vocabulary of lightweight materials that he pioneered in the warm Southern California climate.

ment rather than proposing remedies for social disorder. "What if we simply declare there is not crisis," he asks, "redefine our relationship with the city not as its makers but as its mere subjects, as its supporters?"

Rem Koolhaas and the Office for Metropolitan Architecture (OMA) were chosen to design the master plan of the Euralille complex in November 1988, following the decision to run the high-speed TGV line serving the Channel tunnel through this blighted northern French city (see Chapter 2, Transport and Communications). Physically separated from the rest of the complex designed by Jean Nouvel or

Christian de Portzamparc, Koolhaas's Grand Palais is surrounded by heavily traveled roads. A symphony of unusual, and generally inexpensive, materials ranging from plywood to plastic on the inside, or "fishscale" glass panes on some exterior surfaces, makes this building one of the most interesting examples of contemporary architecture in Europe. Vast (50,000 m² of usable space), and extremely flexible, the Grand Palais does plead in favor of the architectural skills of this Dutch theorist, but it may not fully explain or justify his concept of urban congestion.

Another of the architects chosen for the MoMA exhibition in 1988, Peter Eisenman has had a long career as a theorist, and admittedly has something of a reputation as a troublemaker. One of the so-called "New York Five" with Meier, Hejduk, Stern and Gwathmey in the 1970s, Eisenman has been criticized for frequently changing his architectural ideas. In a scathing article written for the American monthly *Progressive Architecture*, Diane Ghiradro said, "From the early methodology – Eisenman moved rapidly through one infatuation after another: excavations, Boolean cube, Möbius strip, DNA, scaling, or what would appear to be randomly piled strips of cooked fettuccini in the Columbus Convention Center, each of which promised to give structure, order, and diversity to his designs. They also conveniently substituted rational methodology for creative imagination, something that has been a constant in Eisenman's projects."[4]

The "Möbius strip" referred to here is the form of the architect's unbuilt Max Reinhardt Haus project for Berlin. Invented by the German mathematician and

Frank O. Gehry
Vitra International Furniture Manufacturing Facility and Museum
Weil am Rhein, Germany, 1986–89
It remains to be seen if Gehry's expressive manipulation of architectural volumes will really alter the face of contemporary architecture, or if, as he has said himself, it will above all permit younger architects to have greater freedom in creating other types of forms. Named one of America's 25 "most influential people" by *Time Magazine*, Frank O. Gehry has in fact built few large-scale buildings in the United States.

Zaha Hadid
Vitra Fire Station
Weil am Rhein, Germany, 1988–93
Part of the campus of buildings by
exceptional architects brought
together by Vitra chief Rolf Fehl-
baum, Hadid's Fire Station is one
of her first attempts to translate
her spectacular drawings into
built form. Here, despite the surprisingly angular design, interior
space is well managed, creating
a usable and architecturally
spectacular facility. As opposed
to the "frozen motion" of Gehry,
Zaha Hadid's idea of forward
movement is perhaps less lyrical
and more contemporary.

astronomer Augustus Ferdinand Möbius (1790–1868), the strip of the same name
is flat and rectangular, with a half-twist and ends connected to form a continuous-
sided, single-edged loop. Eisenman's proposed double tower is the result of computer "morphing" of a Möbius strip and a projection into three dimensions of its
form. Designed in obvious violation of Berlin height restrictions, the Max Reinhardt
Haus would be located at a major intersection formed by Unter den Linden (east-
west) and Friedrichstrasse (north-south). This site was recognized as pivotal, according to Peter Eisenman, and chosen as a location for potential landmarks such as
the project for the first glass "skyscraper" designed by Mies van der Rohe shortly
after World War I. Named for a famous German theatrical entrepreneur, it would be
built in the same place as his *Schauspielhaus* designed by Hans Poelzig. According to
Eisenman, it would "have a prismatic character, folding into itself, but also opening
itself out to an infinite, always fragmentary, and constantly changing array of metropolitan references and relationships." Eisenman goes on to say, "It will become a
truly prophetic building. Such a structure amounts to a singularity in the city itself,
acquiring the capacity to represent on one site that which is of many places."
Whether it is built or not, the Max Reinhardt Haus represents an apotheosis of
recent trends towards innovative, sculptural computer-generated forms in contemporary architecture.

It is interesting to note that Eisenman, apparently one of the leading lights of the
Deconstructivist movement, today disavows the validity of such analysis for archi-

tecture, preferring to explore the new horizons offered by the computer. As he says, "I believe that deconstruction runs into a big problem, which is its refusal to deal with the physical reality which is presence. Its object is to subvert the metaphysics of presence. You can subvert the metaphysics of drawing, but not of architecture. There will always be four walls in architecture. Rather than arguing against four walls, it is more relevant to argue how you can detach the four walls from a casual perception of architecture. Most people want architecture to remain casual. My work is about making it uncasual. I am interested in internal questions such as those of profile, repetition, movement, of the relation of object to subject perception. This what I would call a fluid architecture. It has a gelatinous quality. We are using a computer technique called morphing. There is very little philosophy that I can read today which is going to help me with the internal problems of memory – that is to say the memory of the computer versus that of the human brain. The random access memory of the computer gives you the enormous possibilities which human mem-

Pages 14/15
Rem Koolhaas
Grand Palais
Lille, France, 1990–94
Part of the Euralille complex of which Koolhaas was the "archi-tect-in-chief," designed around the Lille Europe TGV station, the Grand Palais is a 50,000 m^2 350 million franc convention facility, which makes use of a wide variety of relatively inexpensive materials, such as linoleum floor-ing or corrugated plastic walls. Physically isolated from the rest of Euralille, which was designed by Jean Nouvel, Christian de Portzamparc or Jean-Marie Duthilleul, the Grand Palais is intended to be an expression of Koolhaas's theories of the positive aspects of urban congestion.

ory does not have access to."[5] Beyond Eisenman's current approach, some see even more unusual prospects for the use of the computer in architectural design. As Martin Pearce has written, "The conventional boundary, that of manually inputting data while watching it appear on the screen, is already becoming blurred. In particular, machines are adopting an increasingly biological means of operation..." The term "biological means of operation" refers here to self-replication and development of computer-generated forms, opening the prospect of an architecture without architects.[6]

Bernard Tschumi, born in Lausanne, Switzerland in 1944, was cited in the MoMA show for a project that in many senses remains emblematic of Deconstructivist architecture. His scheme for the La Villette park in northern Paris with its bright red "follies," although only partially completed, is a theoretical exercise that succeeds in reaching out to a large public. As he wrote in 1988, "The park is an elaborate essay in the deviation of ideal forms. It gains its force by turning each distortion of

Pages 16/17
Rem Koolhaas
Grand Palais
Lille, France, 1990–94
Exterior and interior views of the
Grand Palais give an idea of how
the architect has used a variety of
inexpensive materials in an innovative and practical way. One
of the most evident aspects of the
building's design is its capacity
to be readily transformed for
different types of function, from
relatively intimate events to very
large conventions or meetings.

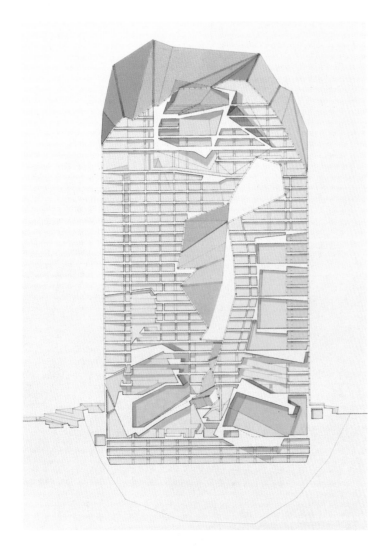

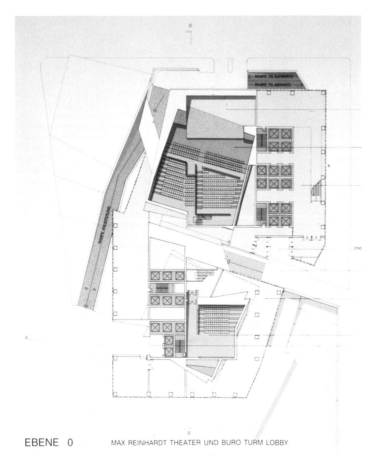

EBENE 0   MAX REINHARDT THEATER UND BÜRO TURM LOBBY

Pages 18/19
Peter Eisenman
Max Reinhardt Haus
Berlin, Germany, 1995 (project)
This project, which remains unbuilt, would clearly violate the
height restrictions that exist in
Berlin, but the architect wanted to
create a "symbolic" structure. The
result of computer "morphing"
of the shape of a Möbius strip,
this connected double tower has
a "crystalline" aspect that the
architect willingly relates to a
difficult episode of German
history. Eisenman insists that
architecture should not make its
users feel comfortable, and
indeed a good part of his *œuvre*
remains in the state of plans.

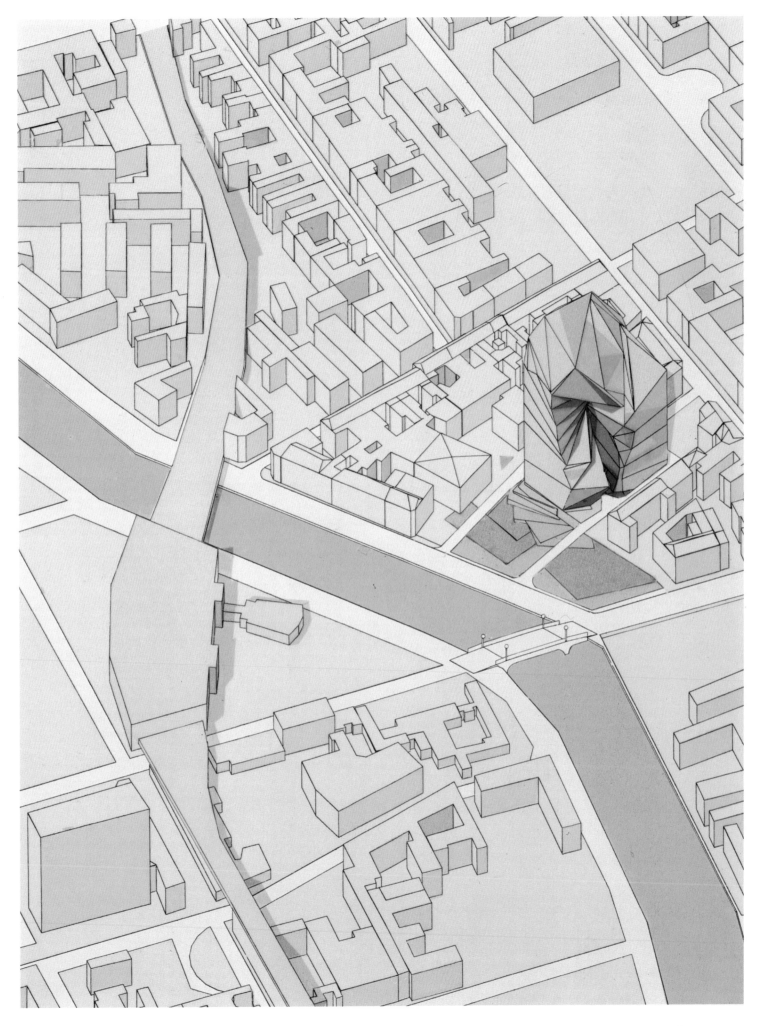

an ideal form into a new ideal, which is then itself distorted. With each new generation of distortion, the trace of the previous ideal remains, producing a convoluted archeology, a history of successive idealizations and distortions. In this way, the park destabilizes pure architectural form."[7] Undeniably sculptural, situated at the very limit of any real usefulness, the Villette follies are certainly a step not only toward "destabilization" but also toward a certain liberation of architecture, which brings the built form closer to art.

One of the most radical of the participants in the 1988 MoMA show, both in rhetorical and formal terms, was the Austrian Coop Himmelblau firm. Perhaps partially because of their uncompromising attitude and the extreme nature of their designs, these architects have not added greatly to their body of built work since their appearance in New York. One of their most notable interventions was in a pavilion designed for the new Groninger Museum in Groningen, The Netherlands. In the unexpected company of Alessandro Mendini, Coop Himmelblau was given the responsibility of creating a space for the museum's collections of traditional paintings. Calling into doubt every possible notion about traditional geometry and museum design, this space may not be an ideal location for Groningen's limited old master collection, but it does prove that the reservoir of astonishing new forms in contemporary architecture is far from being depleted.

The pavilion in question was to be designed by the American artist Frank Stella. Stella's own sculptural forms were abandoned quite late for budgetary reasons, leading Mendini and the museum's director Frans Haks to seek out the Austrians. They had coincidentally built a pavilion almost on the same site for the "What a Wonderful World" exhibition organized in 1990 with Hadid, Eisenman, Koolhaas, and Tschumi, all of whom worked on the concept of locations for the projection of music videos.

The final member of the MoMA seven, the American Daniel Libeskind, has continued work on the Jewish Museum in Berlin, but may not have marked the architectural scene as much as his colleagues in recent years. Despite drifting for the most part from the terrain recognized by Mark Wigley and Philip Johnson as Desconstructivist, all of these architects have explored the relationships between

Pages 20/21
Bernard Tschumi
La Villette "Follies"
Paris, France, 1982–85
The "follies" designed by Tschumi for the gardens of the La Villette park at the periphery of Paris are arranged according to a grid pattern of "decomposed 10 m cubes." They are all painted in the same shade of red, and they share a "deconstructivist" design that makes them almost more sculptural than of any real use, although almost all of them contain some sort of facility. What the structures do with a certain efficiency is to tie together the relatively disparate elements of the park – Christian de Portzamparc's Cité de la Musique, the Grande Halle exhibition building, and the science museum itself.

art and new expressions of the built form. As in art, there may be no dominant esthetic emerging, but rather an uncertainty and a fragmentation of ideas and shapes that quite obviously corresponds to the mood of the times.

It may be that economic factors had a more immediate impact in the United States, where most projects are privately funded, than in Europe, where large state-initiated facilities continued to be launched despite the recession. For various reasons, countries such as France or The Netherlands, with a number of forward-looking mayors and other public officials, came to privilege inventive architects much more than their predecessors did in the 1970s, for example. This, together with the continued fertility of schools such as the AA in London, has apparently led Europe into a position of leadership in creative world architecture, a situation that it had not really had since the early part of the century.

Alessandro Mendini *et al.*
Groninger Museum
Groningen, The Netherlands,
1990–94
A collaborative effort with
Michele de Lucchi, Philip Starck
and Coop Himmelblau, the
Groninger Museum is situated on
the Verbindingskanaal. Recalling
certain Egyptian temples like that
at Philae, it sits in the water, but it
is astride a footbridge connecting
the area of the railway station and
the center of the city. It is thus
an almost obligatory point of
passage for millions of people
every year.

Pages 24/25

Alessandro Mendini *et al.*
Groninger Museum
Groningen, The Netherlands,
1990–94

To the left, the skewed forms of
Coop Himmelblau pavilion have
unexpectedly been chosen to
exhibit the museum's collection
of old master paintings. In the
central part of the structure,
near the 60 m high gold plastic
laminate-covered "treasury"
tower, the bright colors favored
by Mendini rule, whereas
Philippe Starck's area (the silver
drum-shaped section on the image
below) opts for a more muted
color scheme.

Pages 26/27
Alessandro Mendini *et al.*
Groninger Museum
Groningen, The Netherlands,
1990–94
Above, Philippe Starck uses an
undulating curtain as a divider in
his area of the Groninger Museum,
while the Coop Himmelblau
section (right) assumes a much
harder-edged appearance. The
Austrians stepped into the project
at a late stage, after a design by
the artist Frank Stella for the same
pavilion was abandoned as too
costly and complex to build.

California Dreaming

Another region in which circumstances have combined to provoke a great deal of architectural creativity in recent years, is southern California. The presence of Frank O. Gehry in Los Angeles certainly encouraged this activity, but is not the only reason for it. Gehry himself has complained about the lack of real interest for his designs wherever large-scale projects are involved. As he says, "In L.A., I've long been considered strange and odd, a maverick. For years, no big corporation or major developer gave me a commission of any size. Disney Hall, which I won in close competition with Stirling, Hollein and Böhm, is the first big thing I've been given to do in my home town. In Los Angeles, despite all its freedom to experiment, the avantgarde remains peripheral to the mainstream of most of what's being built. I think artistic expression is the juice that fuels our collective souls, that innovation and responding to desperate social needs are not exclusive imperatives." Significantly, his only really large Los Angeles building, the Disney Concert Hall, is on indefinite hold for budgetary reasons.

California architecture has indeed often been most successful when applied to small-scale structures. Because of the presence of the movie industry, and probably because of the "melting pot" nature of the local population, a number of wealthy individuals with a taste for experimentation have called on young, new architects. Fortunately, this willingness to experiment, at least on a small scale, has been matched by the rise of architectural education.

Although USC and UCLA have good architecture programs, one school has stood out over the past years as a crucible for new thinking. The Southern California Institute of Architecture (SCI-Arc), now located on Beethoven Street near Santa Monica, was founded in 1972 by a group that rejected traditional approaches. Amongst them was of course Frank O. Gehry, but his influence has given way to that of Michael Rotondi, former partner with Thom Mayne in Morphosis and now principal of RoTo. According to Rotondi, the idea of SCI-Arc is "to produce architects who are truly artists and thus inherently subversive." Of the faculty of SCI-Arc, Mayne, Rotondi and Eric Owen Moss stand out as some of the most inventive architects of the post-Gehry generation.

The quest of Gehry has centered on formal concerns related to materials, color or design, but the SCI-Arc builders have gone further in thinking out the reasons for the existence of new architectural directions. It should be noted that the inventiveness of southern California architects has depended on a variety of factors that are certainly not reproducible in other parts of the world. A combination of favorable climate with the spectre of natural disaster in the form of unpredicatable earthquakes certainly contributes to their "anything goes" attitude. The latter element (i.e. the fact that the very ground on which architecture is built is not stable) has also relativized the enthusiasm of local designers for technologically oriented solutions, while the fact that California history hardly goes back in any substantive way before 1890 also shapes their willingness to experiment.

Formed in the early 1970s by Mayne and Rotondi, Morphosis has been one of the most influential California architectural practices, again, usually through small-scale projects like their 72 Market Street restaurant (Venice, 1982–85), or the more visible Kate Mantilini restaurant on Wilshire Boulevard in Beverly Hills, whose interior design revolves around a curious sculptural steel object. Mayne calls this sculpture a "useless object," and declares: "Our interest had nothing to do with the restaurant function, but rather with creating a public space which would reverberate, between the individual and the automobile." Intensely intellectual, with a meandering style of expression, Thom Mayne explains his approach to architecture: "The business of architecture serves clients. You go out there and you find out what clients need today – what are they interested in today? Real architecture is the antithesis of that. Your interests are more private and personal over an extended

Page 29
Morphosis
Kate Mantilini Restaurant
Beverly Hills, California, 1987
The image to the upper right shows the sign on the facade of the actual restaurant, while the photo of the model below was taken in the Santa Monica offices of the architects. The precise nature of the model is one aspect of the work of this group, whose leader is Thom Mayne. Although the Kate Mantilini Restaurant functions well as a crowded, fashionable eating spot, its design is such that the space could undoubtedly serve other functions just as well.

Pages 30/31
Eric Owen Moss
Gary Group Building,
Paramount Laundry Building
Culver City, California, 1987–90
Part of an ongoing effort to
renovate underused or abandoned
buildings in the Los Angeles area
of Culver City, this group of three
buildings, situated around a
parking lot that may eventually be
the site of another Moss project
(Ince Theater), demonstrate the
inventiveness of a new generation
of California architects.

Pages 32/33
Eric Owen Moss
The Box
Culver City, California, 1990–94
Located on a main thoroughfare in Culver City, this structure, with its rooftop addition called a "bronco attic" by the architect, is near to the 8522 National Boulevard Building and the Goalen Group, which Eric Owen Moss restructured in 1988–90, as well as the more recent IRS Building. All of these are part of the so-called Hayden Tract, which Moss and developer Frederick Norton Smith have been rehabilitating for most of the past ten years.

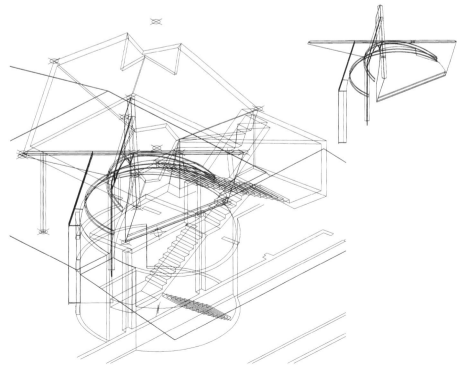

Pages 34/35
Eric Owen Moss
Lawson-Westen House
Los Angeles, California, 1988–93
This private home, located in the
Brentwood area, is one of the few
entirely new structures designed
by Moss. By including references
to the design process in the house
itself, the architect creates a built
equivalent of "pentimenti" in
painting. At once innovative and
practical in its use of unusual
shapes, the Lawson-Westen
House confirms the considerable
architectural talent of Eric Owen
Moss.

period of time and require an independence which is akin to leadership. It is up to
you to define the issues. I am not interested in fashion or even in the look of the
work. I am interested in starting ideas that take you someplace, and in the process,
in the methodological process. You have to build to get feedback. Some people
start with the visual or physiognomic characteristics. They work towards manifest-
ing that vision. I don't work that way. I work with concepts that build to something.
I don't know where I am going. Materials are chosen very late. It has to do with lines
and directions and forces which have nothing to do with appearance. It is not easy
to deal with clients because most of them are not at all interested in the investigation. The solution is a process of getting to a further or deeper analysis of
the problem. People react to architecture in stylistic terms, but making architecture
has to do with the invention of something that contains its own power and beauty
– its own authenticity. Laying a few things on top of each other isn't enough. Out
of that has to come some sort of invention. The process of actually making follows
the invention. It is that first part which is more difficult. I start with complete
blackness."[8]

A third SCI-Arc faculty member of interest is Eric Owen Moss. Born in Los Angeles in 1943, educated at UCLA, he opened his own office in Culver City in 1976, and a peculiarity of his work is that most of it is situated in that area of the city. Through his affiliation with a developer based in Culver City, located midway between downtown Los Angeles and Santa Monica, Moss has had the opportunity to build complexes that incrementally connect together, such as the Paramount Laundry-Lindblade Tower-Gary Group Complex, completed between 1987 and 1990. More recent rehabilitation of these large warehouse-type structures, originally built for the movie industry, includes The Box and IRS buildings, located nearby. Making very inventive use of common materials such as sewer pipes serving as columns, or bolts bent in a U shape to form a fluorescent light fixture, Moss has managed to create an impetus for forward-looking advertising or recording companies to install themselves in an area that was all but abandoned a few years ago. The architect Philip Johnson has dubbed him "the jeweler of junk." Like Mayne, Moss projects an intensely intellectual approach to his designs, relating them to his understanding of the state of the world in an interesting manner. As Moss says, "T.S. Eliot wrote about 'the still point of the turning world.' Lao Tse wrote about 'the square with no corners.' You can't have a square with no corners, can you? If a building represents fixity, then it represents a particular condition or an understanding at a particular point in time. But if the architecture itself could include oppositions, so that the building itself as an aspiration was about movement or the movement of ideas, then it might be more durable. It would embody something that would move notwithstanding the fact that it represents something which physiologically is fixed."[9] This theoretical stance is given form in an architecture that conserves reminiscences of its own design process, as is the case in the 1993 Lawson-Westen House, in the fashionable Brentwood section of Los Angeles. Like The Box, this residence pursues nothing else than a redefinition of architectural space. Perhaps less

computer-oriented than Eisenman and some others, Eric Owen Moss has nonetheless taken on the rectilinear box of Modernism in a remarkable way, whether it be in his warehouse renovations or, more dramatically, in new construction like the house.

As is the case of a number of other structures designed in the so-called Deconstructivist style, the 1988 Steel Cloud, West Coast Gateway project, for Los Angeles, has yet to be built. The 1988 Los Angeles Gateway Competition, organized by Nick Patsaouras, drew some 200 entries. The winning design was submitted by the young New York architects Lise Anne Couture and Hani Rashid. Their 500 m linear structure was intended to cross an eight-lane freeway with an "episodic architecture inspired by optical machinery, simulators, surveillance technologies and telecommunication systems." A highly symbolic architectural gesture, the Steel Cloud was conceived as a clear signal that Los Angeles has replaced New York as the "Ellis Island of the 1990s." Metaphorically it is a deconstruction of the Statue of Liberty, or perhaps of Tatlin's Monument to the Third International, and although it was portrayed in the media as a folly, this project, which includes numerous screens to project information or movies, represents the recuperation of a dead space over a sunken freeway. Intended as a privately financed project, the Steel Cloud, long delayed, may still one day be built.

Once again, by calling on forms that are quite far from the ordinary experience of architecture, while still having their links with the history of art and design, Rashid and Couture have imagined a way to expand the horizons of the built form while calling too on the varied influences of the "information society."

The rather free experimentation in architecture nurtured by the benevolent southern California climate may be coming at least to a temporary close. Continued economic retrenchment in the 1990s has made many potential clients look much more carefully at their architectural options. Stunning excess is clearly no longer the name of the game. More, as Peter Eisenman says, "The world has changed. It has all become very conservative."[10]

France and the Return of Europe

One of the reasons for the exceptional creativity of European architecture in recent years has certainly been an acceptance by governments at the federal, regional and local levels that a high quality of design is compatible with the requirements of public accounting. Naturally, such initiatives are much rarer as economic conditions become more difficult, and they always depend on the attitudes of specific leaders.

In this respect, the fourteen years of rule of François Mitterrand in France, from 1981 to 1995, had a marked influence on architecture. Not only did his government launch numerous large-scale projects (the *Grands Travaux*), ranging from I.M. Pei's Louvre Pyramid to an opera house at the Bastille, but every effort was made to call on the best international architects. Occasionally this process went awry, but for the most part it can be concluded that Mitterrand succeeded not only in adding substantial contemporary monuments to Paris, but also in encouraging other authorities to think in similar terms. The *Grands Travaux* also brought to the forefront a variety of younger talents, from Jean Nouvel (Institut du Monde Arabe) to Christian de Portzamparc, winner of the 1994 Pritzker Prize, and author of the Cité de la Musique, situated at the northern periphery of Paris.

Known for his lyrical forms, criticized by some as being overly complex, Christian de Portzamparc's reputation certainly spread beyond France quite quickly. One of his current projects, a tower for the Bandai toy company in Tokyo, shows that his style has evolved considerably, perhaps under the influence of computer-aided design. The intensive research that he has undertaken to permit an almost infinite variety of modifications of the light patterns on this structure is related to his work on the inside of the main concert hall of the Cité de la Musique. Another French talent who came to the fore in the 1980s is Philippe Starck. Known first as a furniture and interior designer, he has gone on to build a number of buildings, especially in Japan, like his curious Baron Vert building in Osaka (1992), wedged between a busy street and a graveyard. There is a natural relation between Starck's rather futuristic objects and his object-like buildings. Taking a point of departure that is clearly different than that of most architects, Starck nonetheless figures in a wider effort to redefine the very shapes of buildings. It is interesting to note that despite the recent opening of the attitude of the French toward contemporary architecture, Starck feels that he is not accepted as an architect in his own country. Indeed his project for an addition to the Paris Ecole d'arts décoratifs has encountered local opposition.

Though there is not a specific link between the *Grands Travaux* of François Mitterrand and the ambitious expansion of the French National Railroads (SNCF), a similar interest in the quality of architecture has been evidenced in their program related to high-speed train lines (TGV). Most of the new stations are in-house projects designed essentially by Jean-Marie Duthilleul, but the Lyon-Satolas station at Lyon airport is a notable exception. Here, the Spanish engineer Santiago Calatrava has created a 5,600 m² structure whose main terminal area resembles a bird in flight. Calatrava's station evidently echoes Eero Saarinen's TWA Terminal at Kennedy Airport (1957–62) in its suggestion of a bird in flight, but it is more exuberant than its American ancestor.

One Paris region town with a new RER station designed by Jean-Marie Duthilleul is Cergy-Le-Haut. This is also the location for one of the more spectacular and futuristic high schools recently built anywhere. The Lycée Jules Verne, named after the science-fiction author, is the work of Architecture Studio, who were partners of Nouvel for the Institut du Monde Arabe project. Like a spacecraft in its wedge-shaped configuration, this building provides further evidence of creativity even in an environment of severely restricted official budgets.

Although examples of innovative architecture are to be found in several European countries, and will be dealt with elsewhere in this volume, it should be

Pages 38/39
Christian de Portzamparc
Bandai Cultural Complex
Tokyo, Japan, 1994 (project)
This 7,000 m² tower, to include a theater, offices, housing and a restaurant, which remains unbuilt, would have a facade that would change colors using a system similar to that employed by the architect in the concert hall of the Cité de la Musique in Paris.

emphasized again here that aside from France, The Netherlands may be one of the most committed proponents of contemporary forms on the old continent. The Groninger Museum in Groningen, cited above because of its Coop Himmelblau designed pavilion, is in fact an accumulation of the work of several designers under the direction of Alessandro Mendini. Philippe Starck for one was responsible for the section having to do with the museum's ceramics collection. Like Starck, Mendini is far better known for his design work than he is for architecture. Modeling his museum on the Egyptian temple of Philae, situated on an artificial island in the canal separating the central train station from the town center, this surprising structure is now an almost obligatory point of reference for all those seeking to enter this northern Dutch city. Built thanks to the generosity of the Netherlands Gasunie company, the Groninger Museum is an outstanding example of collaboration between political, corporate, architectural and museum personalities.

Above
Architecture Studio
Lycée Jules Verne
Cergy-Le-Haut, France, 1991–93
This is a 16,600 m² facility built for 1,350 pupils with a budget of 108 million French francs. Architecture Studio was chosen in a 1991 competition organized by the Ile de France Regional Council. The cylindrical building in the main body of the futuristic triangle houses staff facilities, and a series of bridges join the different volumes together.

Right
Philippe Starck
La Flamme
Asahi Breweries, Tokyo, Japan,
1990
Built for the Asahi Breweries,
this building created considerable
controversy when it was built.
Starck also designed the interiors
which include a restaurant and
bar.

Eastern Stars

The property boom of the 1980s made Japan one of the most propitious places in the world for the development of architecture. Extraordinary prosperity, coupled with a very high quality of construction and, in some quarters at least, an appreciation for the virtues of contemporary architecture, permitted such figures as Arata Isozaki or Tadao Ando to build more than most of their Western colleagues. Naturally, when the property "bubble" burst, it was discovered that many real estate developers were in serious financial straits, and excess capacity replaced feverish construction. Despite these handicaps, a number of very talented Japanese architects have continued to define international standards in their exploration of new forms, which also very frequently have deep links to the traditions of their country. Three projects completed since 1993 give an indication of this continued presence.

Itsuko Hasegawa is one of the few women to have successfully made her way in the largely male-dominated world of architecture and construction. In her computer-filled Tokyo offices, she has conceived a number of the more innovative designs seen anywhere in recent years. Her Sumida Culture Factory, completed in September 1994 in Tokyo, is an 8,000 m² "public hall, library and workshop." It is a five-story building with a reinforced concrete and steel frame structure, which addresses the Japanese interest in an impression of extreme lightness, especially through its envelope of translucent perforated aluminum screens. Indeed the lightness of this design is at least partially a response to local earthquake conditions.

Another architect preoccupied with lightness, and with the substantial impact of the "information society" on architecture, is Toyo Ito. His 1993 Shimosuwa Lake Suwa Museum, located in Nagano, is constituted by two separate volumes – a cube on the mountain side and a long linear form on the lake side positioned on a 200 m by 400 m site. The lakeside volume forms a streamlined aluminum-clad curve inspired by the designer's original image of a "boat floating on the lake." According to the architect, "Structural elements and utility fixtures are incorporated into the walls to avoid any protuberances. Both the aluminum panels and the ceiling boards are independent of the body of the structure, covering the gentle curve of the building like a second skin." Somewhat less complex than Hasegawa's Sumida Culture Factory, the Lake Suwa Museum is a clear indication of Toyo Ito's mastery of what must surely be called the emerging forms in contemporary architecture. Once again, designs such as complex curves have only become conceivable for limited budget public architecture in recent years thanks to computer-aided design and manufacturing. As Nancy Solomon wrote in the magazine *Architecture*, "forward-thinking architects are now capitalizing on 'computer-aided design/computer-aided manufacturing (CAD/CAM)' to produce highly detailed building designs and unconventional geometric forms at reasonable costs." She continues to say, "CAD/CAM means more than the fabrication of repetitive elements. In the field of architecture, where each final product is unique, CAM also facilitates a more complex, dynamic process in which sophisticated three-dimensional computer models of projects are made available to contractors and their subcontractors as informational tools to clarify fabrication, whether by traditional or robotic techniques. With such software, the architect can document complex, irregular shapes and generate more detailed construction documents for the fabricator. As a result, the practitioner not only broadens creative opportunities, but also streamlines the construction process while maintaining stronger control over design."[11]

A third figure who must be cited here is Fumihiko Maki, a true aristocrat in the world of Japanese architecture, and one of the most international figures currently working in Tokyo. His Kirishima Concert Hall is on the Kirishima Plateau on the southernmost island of Kyushu. Especially by the usual Japanese standards of urban congestion, this site is remarkably pristine. The Kirishima peaks stand to the east,

Page 43
Itsuko Hasegawa
Sumida Culture Factory
Tokyo, Japan, 1992–94
The basic drawings for this building, which is located in a busy central area of Tokyo, were created using CAD (computer-aided design), together with manual drafting and model building, a combination that Hasegawa, the best-known contemporary Japanese female architect, finds particularly efficient.

Pages 44/45
Itsuko Hasegawa
Sumida Culture Factory
Tokyo, Japan, 1992–94
Wrapped in "multiple layers of translucent membranes," the Sumida Culture Factory consists of three wings situated around a central plaza. The reinforced concrete structure with a steel frame is five stories high and includes 8,447 m² of floor space on a 3,400 m² site.

and Sakura Island can be seen to the south, creating a superb natural panorama. As is often the case in Fumihiko Maki's most successful designs, there is a subtle mixture here between references to tradition and a futuristic form. The faceted irregularity of the roof over the 800-seat concert hall stands out with its aluminum sheen from the natural background, more like a precious jewel than like an intrusion on the environment.

In Japan, as in California or Western Europe, an active search is under way for new forms in architecture. Assisted by the computer, and liberated both from the interdiction to make reference to the past that went with Modernism, and from the superficial pastiche-type designs of Post-Modernism, architects have done nothing less than begin to challenge the very form of the built environment. By seeking out new forms that are undeniably sculptural, these architects have done much to affirm the movement of which Frank O. Gehry will be remembered as a pioneer, toward the return of architecture to its status as one of the fine arts. As is always the case, a certain amount of fruitless experimentation is to be expected in such circumstances, but the facility introduced by the widespread use of computer assisted design makes it very likely that the unusual curves and facets seen in these pages will have a profound impact on the wider circle of architects who indeed design most of the buildings in typical cities around the world.

Toyo Ito
Shimosuwa Lake Suwa Museum
Shimosuwa-machi, Nagano, Japan,
1990–93
The entrance of the museum looks
out onto the lake. Its design is
typical of the light almost ethereal
style of Toyo Ito.

Toyo Ito
Shimosuwa Lake Suwa Museum
Shimosuwa-machi, Nagano, Japan,
1990–93

The site of this museum is 200 m long, but very narrow, and situated between a four-lane prefectural highway and a band including railroad tracks and another road. Toyo Ito imagined his structure in the shape of an over-turned boat, complete with an emerging concrete rudder at the rear. Despite the relatively literal nature of this reference, Ito has made the overall form sufficiently abstract for it to be quite spectacular.

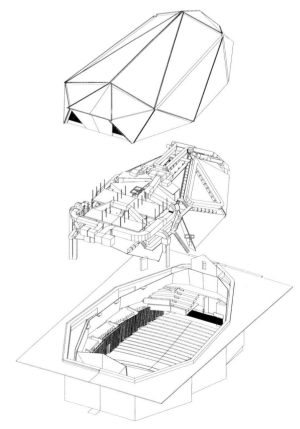

Pages 48/49
Fumihiko Maki
Kirishima Concert Hall
Aira, Kagoshima, Japan, 1993–94
Set on a 4.8 ha site in a range of
volcanic mountains on the island
of Kyushu, the Kirishima Concert
Hall is a 4,904 m^2 facility that is
intended as the basis for a future
cultural park in Kirishima, which
each year hosts an internationally
recognized music festival.
An outdoor amphitheater with
seating for 4,000 spectators is one
feature of this complex, which is
centered on the main concert hall,
seating 770.

URBAN STRATEGIES

Transport, Communications, Tall Buildings and the Urban Nomad

Continuing urbanization, particularly in the developing world, has naturally fueled the evolution of architecture. The most significant emerging trend in this respect has of course been the remarkable economic progress registered by a number of Asian economies, stretching from Korea to Indonesia. The need for massive new construction does not often go hand in hand with quality architecture; indeed the opposite is quite often the case. Because this book is concerned with seeking out exceptions to this rule, it should be pointed out that one criterion of economic success is, after all, the capacity to call on architects of worldwide reputation. Japan and Hong Kong have reached out in this respect, and other nations such as China or Malaysia are now following suit. Like Chicago and New York in another era, Shanghai or Kuala Lumpur are competing to see which city can build the highest, most spectacular towers, a notion that seemed almost outdated in recent years in the West. The boom in Asia has even more significant impact, because the economies concerned are seeking to skip a number of the steps that Western countries made on the way to their own prosperity. Transport and communications are an essential part of this equation, and in the latter category the rapid progress of electronics and data transmission through computers and such techniques as fiber-optics make it entirely conceivable that certain new trading powers could suddenly stand out among the most modern countries in the world. Aside from Japan, which is already in a more mature phase of development, many Asian nations do still look to the West for advice and assistance in these areas, because the pace of their expansion is such that they have not had time to work out all of their own strategies.

The United States has certainly played a leading role in the spreading use of computers, but it may be that Europe has been more forward-looking in the infrastructure of transport and communications. Indeed with antiquated airports such as Kennedy in New York and a rail system whose passenger capacity has not been significantly improved in a very long time, the United States looks more and more like an aging power as compared with the more forward-looking attitude exhibited by countries such as France. It is no accident that Korea is looking to a use of France's high-speed TGV rail system, or that European architects have been called on to design enormous new facilities such as the Kansai Airport (Renzo Piano), the new Hong Kong airport (Sir Norman Foster), or the planned 170,000 m² Kowloon train station by Terry Farrell.

Transport and Communications

No project is more emblematic of the resurgence of transportation and communication in architecture than the extraordinary new Kansai airport built by the Italian Renzo Piano on an artificial island in the bay of Osaka. Despite the examples of Dulles Airport in Washington, D.C., or the TWA Terminal building at Kennedy Airport (1957–62), both by Eero Saarinen, until about ten years ago few countries took the architecture of their airports very seriously. Like railway stations, airports

were anonymous points of transition, where architecture mattered less than simply moving people in and out with as little fuss as possible. The rapid development of the Asian economies and their reliance on worldwide air transport have been one factor in the change of this attitude. In fact, the idea of locating the airport on the sea in the Kansai (Kyoto-Osaka) area was first proposed in 1971, as a response both to the density of local construction and to the need to keep flights landing or taking off 24 hours a day despite strict noise regulations. The resulting structure is a feat of engineering and architecture that has few equals in history. An island, 4.37 km long and 1.27 km wide, was quite simply created on the 18 m deep seabed, requiring the use of no less than 180 million m³ of landfill. This 511 ha island, a "platform born at the juncture of the sea and the sky," was the object of an international competition in November 1988, which brought together fifteen groups of architects and builders, including such well-known names as Sir Norman Foster, Ricardo Bofill, I.M. Pei, Kazuhiro Ishii, Jean Nouvel, Kiyonori Kikutake, and Bernard Tschumi. The winner, Renzo Piano, designed a "megastructure" 1.7 km long as the main passenger terminal. As large as this building seems, in the imagination of the architect it was only part of a much bigger ring with a diameter of 16.4 km, tilted at an angle of 68.2° with respect to the surface. The terminal was imagined as that portion of the ring that is exposed above ground. The roof of the completed building measures no less than 90,000 m², covered by 82,400 identical ferrite-type stainless steel panels, whose weather resistance is close to that of titanium. Despite numerous difficulties, including the ongoing "problem of differential settlement," which simply put means that parts of the artificial island are settling faster than others, the Kansai project is no doubt exemplary of the kind of international cooperation that such huge projects will engender in the future. Together with the Italian architect, the French group Aéroports de Paris (Paul Andreu) developed the basic concept; Nikken Sekkei was responsible for the foundations, the first and second floors; Bechtel and Fluor Daniel of the United States acted as general contractors, and Watson of Great

Pages 54/55
Renzo Piano
Kansai International Airport
Osaka, Japan, 1988–95
Built on a 511 ha artificial island, a "platform born at the juncture of the sea and the sky," this remarkable airport was the object of an international competition in November 1988, which brought together fifteen groups of architects and builders. The winner, Renzo Piano, designed a "megastructure" 1.7 km long as the main passenger terminal.

Britain and Eiffel of France as subcontractors. Another huge Asian project is the new airport at Chek Lap Kok currently being built by Sir Norman Foster, which is intended to handle upwards of 40 million passengers a year before the end of the decade. Confirming the trend, the new Seoul Metropolitan Airport (Fentress Bradburn/BHJW), located on Yong Jong Do Island in the Yellow Sea, 50 km west of Seoul, is also due for completion in the year 2000.

Although airports of the past never underwent the kind of architectural transformation being wrought at this moment by Asian ambitions coupled with Western architectural talent, railway stations used to aspire to palatial dimensions. According to Jean-Marie Duthilleul, head architect of the French national railways (SNCF), it was a combination of factors, including the devastation of World War II and the rise of the airplane, which condemned the great European train stations built between the late nineteenth century and the 1930s. Duthilleul is presently

heading an effort in France to give stations back some of the excitement they lost when it was decided that underground, anonymous spaces would do for a type of transport that seemed to be condemned by the airborne competition. In fact, the TGV *(train à grande vitesse)* lines that the French government has invested in heavily in the past decade have brought about a transformation not only in station architecture, but also in the property development that accompanies the creation of the new, high-speed lines. The most significant example of this trend has occurred along the Eurostar line, which links Paris to London via the Channel Tunnel. Duthilleul's group has revamped the formerly sinister Gare du Nord into a friendly, efficient point of departure. He is also responsible for the new Lille-Europe station, which is at the heart of the so-called Euralille development. It was thanks to the political clout of former Prime Minister Pierre Mauroy, the mayor of Lille since 1973,

Pages 56/57
Jean-Marie Duthilleul
Lille-Europe Railway Station
Lille, France, 1990–94
The very justification of the
Euralille complex, of which Rem
Koolhaas was the "architect-in-
chief," was the arrival of the rapid
TGV train line connecting Paris,
Brussels and London via the

Channel tunnel. Open and bright,
the station features a 500 m
long undulating roof, where
towers by Christian de
Portzamparc and Claude
Vasconi are perched.

that his blighted northern city was included at the last moment in the route to London in the place of Amiens. Suddenly, Lille was to find itself only one hour from Paris by train, and two hours from London. Lille-Europe would become an obligatory point of passage for some 30 million passengers a year. Significantly, Margaret Thatcher and François Mitterrand signed the agreement to build the TGV-tunnel link in the Lille mayor's office in January 1986. Rem Koolhaas (OMA) was chosen to oversee the development of the multi-use Euralille complex, combining the train station, a 155,000 m² commercial center, two office towers, and the 50,000 m² Grand Palais convention center (see the Introduction), in November 1988. Koolhaas, who has become a true "star" of international architecture, was quick to grasp the significance of this massive urban development project, which was in fact an integral part of a system of transportation. "The underlying notion," he said, "is that you don't look at distance anymore, but at the time it takes to go from one place to another. 60 to 70 million people now live within 90 minutes of each other. By the sheer fluke of geography, Lille is the transplanted heart of a virtual community." Rather than being based on more traditional definitions of place, the architecture and development of the future could thus depend on the location of nodal points in the web being created by new forms of transport and communications.

Pages 58/59
Nicholas Grimshaw
Waterloo International Terminal
London, Great Britain, 1990–93
Snaking its way through a rather unpleasant section of London not far from the South Bank complex, which includes the Hayward Gallery, the form of the new Waterloo Terminal was in part dictated by technical factors such as the turning radius of Eurostar trains. Bright and airy, especially on the train platforms themselves, Waterloo provides a fitting complement to the new French stations on the same line.

Although the influence of the French projects may only be peripheral in this instance, the English end of the Eurostar line is marked by another significant piece of architecture, Nicholas Grimshaw's extension to Waterloo Station in London. In the desolate South Bank area, where car and rail traffic have all but excluded pedestrians, Grimshaw's long curved snake of a building brings a touch of color and light that recalls the great tradition of Paxton or Eiffel. This "gateway to Europe" is intended to handle upwards of 15 million passengers a year, and to have a life of a century. Again, the ambition and scale of this effort herald a new type of architecture, even if British Rail has fallen years behind in the construction of the high-speed rail lines that give breath to the Eurostar project. The prospect of a renewal of the South Bank complex may well be speeded now that the Waterloo terminal is operational, giving the whole area a concentration of cultural and communications facilities unparalleled in London. The message here, as in the Euralille complex, may be that good architects are now considered a commercial asset, capable not only of respecting a budget but of inciting public or even official interest to a greater extent than more ordinary practitioners.

The idea of a new type of architecture designed to meet the needs of evolving transportation nodes is confirmed by the remarkable bird-like structure designed by the Spanish engineer Santiago Calatrava for the Lyon-Satolas station, where the south-bound TGV lines meet the Lyon airport. 120 m long, 100 m wide and 40 m high, this "bird" is made of 1,300 tons of steel, resting on two concrete arches. Although the suggestion of flight evoked by the building may recall Eero Saarinen's TWA Terminal, Calatrava's imagery is more dramatic, confirming his place as one of the most creative contemporary architect/engineers, in the spirit of Italian Pier Luigi Nervi or the Swiss bridge designer Robert Maillart.

Transportation and communication have also come to inspire structures that do not function as part of a visible architectural complex, but rather as elements in the growing, invisible network of electronics. Such is certainly the case of Sir Norman

Foster's Torre de Collserola, described by the City of Barcelona as a "monumental technological element" when he won the competition in May 1988. This 288 m high telecommunications tower dominates the city, recalling that the architectural history of the city did not stop with the towers of Gaudí's Sagrada Familia. Foster, whose architectural practice is amongst the most successful in Europe, indeed seems to be at his best when he is facing a technical problem that enables him to use all of his considerable ingenuity. He points out with pride that a conventional tower this height would require a supporting shaft 25 m in diameter, whereas the Torre de Collserola has a 4.5 m diameter "hollow slip-formed reinforced concrete main shaft," which reduces to a minuscule 300 mm at the base of the upper radio mast.

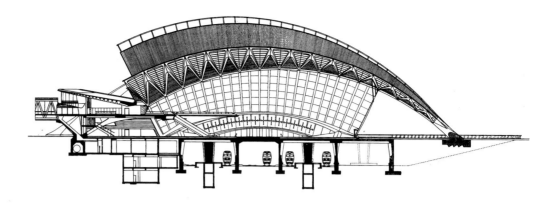

Pages 60/61
Santiago Calatrava
Lyon-Satolas Railway Station
Lyon, France, 1989–94

Intended for rapid TGV trains, Calatrava's bird-like terminal with its connecting link to the Satolas Airport is one of the most spectacular examples of this Spanish engineer/architect's use of forms inspired by nature to create new architectural designs. Although the work of predecessors of Calatrava such as Pier Luigi Nervi is brought to mind, the very energy contained in this structure sets it apart.

Tall Buildings

Although it is clearly in Asia that the concept of the very tall building is being given a new lease on life, the demand for such structures still exists in the West. The true urban density required to make tall buildings economically viable in the most obvious sense probably does not exist in very many cities. Indeed, the logic behind the tower may often be one related to the ego of its builders. An obvious symbol of success or power, towers will tomorrow mark the contemporary Asian city much as they did the American metropolis throughout the twentieth century. As Paul Goldberger has written, "Surely more than any other type of building, the skyscraper is both quintessentially American and quintessentially of the twentieth century. It emerged in the nineteenth century and owes a certain debt to European architecture, but it was in the United States in the first four decades of this century that the skyscraper became not a curiosity of commercial architecture, but a bold force, a force as powerful in its ability to transform the urban environment in its time as the automobile was to be in the decades succeeding."[12]

Though it may not be the most typical example of the American skyscraper, one New York project, Arquitectonica's 1995 42nd Street building, will be cited here simply to demonstrate the continued vitality of this building type in the United States. A cooperative venture of the Disney Corporation and the Tishman Urban Development Corporation, this multi-building complex, meant to symbolize the rebirth of Times Square, is scheduled to open on January 1, 2000. Located at the corner of Eighth Avenue and 42nd Street, the building is designed to look like an exploding meteor. Arquitectonica, who won this project in a competition over Michael Graves and Zaha Hadid, will design a forty-seven-story tower for a

Sir Norman Foster
Torre de Collserola
Barcelona, Spain, 1988–92
Conscious of the architectural heritage of Barcelona and of the highly visible hilltop location of this telecommunications tower, Foster has placed great emphasis on the extremely light nature of his intervention. This is a modernity in tune with the far-reaching impact not only of telecommunications but also with a society which is more and more dominated by electronics in general.

Arquitectonica
Times Square Building
New York, New York, 1995–2000

A confirmation of the rising reputation of the young Miami-based architects Bernardo Fort-Brescia and Laurinda Spear, this tower, designed as though a comet was crashing into it, brings together the imagery of popular culture and a hard-headed sense of business, an apt combination when dealing with large corporate clients such as Disney and Tishman Urban Development.

680-room hotel sheathed in colored glass, like the curving tail of the meteor. A retail and entertainment complex closer to ground level will be covered with "supersigns," and a tower of video monitors will mark the entrance of the hotel on the corner of Eighth Avenue. *The New York Times* called this project "an apocalypse with room service," but it seems evident that the animation desired by the clients for this difficult site has been achieved by Arquitectonica. The apparently chaotic appearance of the lower levels was designed by the architects as an echo of the highly commercial and occasionally dangerous surrounding streets. With this project, if it is successfully completed, Arquitectonica will not only prove its ability to work in the very particular environment of Manhattan with major corporate clients, but also, hopefully, show that intriguing modern architecture can have a beneficial impact on urban blight.

Japan has not been given to the construction of tall buildings, mainly for geological reasons. Aside from certain areas in Tokyo, where towers can be anchored in bedrock, for example, the necessary earthquake resistance cannot be readily obtained. A remarkable exception to this rule is Hiroshi Hara's 1993 Umeda Sky City in Osaka. Hara's notion of "Interconnected Superskyscrapers" goes beyond his own double tower to imagine the creation of a "three-dimensional city network," where numerous tall structures would be linked by skybridges. The extravagant appearance of the Umeda Sky building also translates Hara's dreams about the future of architecture. As he writes, "Architecture must accommodate the electronics age and be directed toward the future. Machine-like buildings were the goal of architecture in the first half of this century, but today's aim is to simulate electronics. The greatest impact electronics has had on our lives is through its fusion of fiction and reality. The microchip erases distance and eliminates the barriers of time... Buildings of the electronics age must be like space stations generating new fictions and nurturing new sensibilities worldwide."[13]

Another twin tower connected by a skybridge complex, designed by the Argentine/American architect Cesar Pelli, is located in the Kuala Lumpur City

Pages 64/65
Hiroshi Hara
Umeda Sky City
Kita-ku, Osaka, Japan, 1988–93
This forty-story, 173 m high double tower, with its two sections 54 m apart, features a "Floating Garden" 150 m above the ground. A 6 m wide steel bridge at the twenty-second level also links the buildings. Hiroshi Hara calls this an "interconnected super-skyscraper." He says, "We must develop and practice living in a variety of high-density modes."

Cesar Pelli
Petronas Towers
Kuala Lumpur, Malaysia, 1991–96
Winner of an invited international
competition for Phase One of the
Kuala Lumpur City Center project,
Cesar Pelli designed these twin
451 m high towers, which are the
tallest office buildings in the
world. Set in a development area
of some 45 ha, formerly the site
of the Selangor Turf Club in the
heart of the commercial district
or "Golden Triangle," the towers
are eighty-eight stories high, and
are linked at the forty-first floor
by a 58 m skybridge.

Center, whose first phase is scheduled for 1996 completion. To meet the demand
for urban growth of the Malaysian capital, the Selangor Turf Club and its surrounding land, some 45 ha in the heart of the commercial district or "Golden Triangle"
were freed for the construction of a new "city within a city." The twin eighty-eight-
story, 451 m high Petronas Towers are connected by a skybridge at the forty-first
floor to facilitate inter-tower communication and traffic. Boasting a GDP growth of
8.4 percent in 1994, Malaysia's is one of the fastest expanding economies in the
world, and the Petronas Towers will certainly mark Kuala Lumpur as a center to be
reckoned with in the years to come.

Another tower, also in Kuala Lumpur, deserves to be considered here, even if its
total height of only fifteen stories does not place it in the same category of many of

Ken Yeang
Menara Mesiniaga
Kuala Lumpur, Malaysia, 1990–92
This fifteen-story corporate headquarters of an IBM franchise,
designed for low energy consumption, is the result of long research
by the architect into the idea of
what he calls the "bioclimatic"
building, specifically suited to a
tropical climate. This building
was a recipient of the 1995 Aga
Khan Award.

the other tall buildings being erected in Asia. Indeed, it would seem that the architect, Ken Yeang, is opposed to Kuala Lumpur's own tendency to want to reach for
the sky. His Menara Mesiniaga, completed in 1992, is the headquarters of an IBM
franchise in Subang Jaya on the outskirts of the Malaysian capital. This tower, one
of the twelve recipients of the 1995 Aga Khan Award for Architecture, is a prototype of what the architect calls a "bioclimatic tall building." Two spirals of green
"sky gardens" twist up the building and provide shade and visual contrast with the
steel and aluminum surfaces. Core functions are placed on the warmer eastern side
of the building, and sunscreens permit a more frugal use of energy. As Peter
Eisenman, a member of the 1995 Aga Khan Award jury, said: "Here we have an
example of a replicable corporate high-rise building that is environmentally sensit-

ive to local discourse, and is also forward looking."[14] Simply put, not everyone agrees that very tall buildings are a viable urban solution, and some architects, like Ken Yeang in Kuala Lumpur, have sought to improve at very least the negative environmental impact that such buildings can have.

Because of China's massive population, its growth will surely influence its region and the world more than that of smaller countries. The relatively recent arrival of an almost capitalist system there has already given rise to numerous spectacular architectural projects. The New York firm HLW International is, for example, responsible for the proposed 516 m high Chongqing Office Tower. Located just west of the juncture of the Yangtze and Jialing Rivers, this structure would be 43 m taller than the Sears Tower in Chicago, making the point that this western Chinese commercial center has now arrived in the league of the great cities.

Chongqing may not in fact win the competition to build the tallest building in China, as other, more likely candidates emerge. Another American firm, Skidmore, Owings & Merrill, has designed a 419 m skyscraper for Shanghai. With nearly 20 million persons expected to be living there early in the next century, Shanghai has plans to build over 10 million m² of new space by 2010, a good part of it in the new Pudong area. Although other American architects, like Kohn Pederson Fox, also have projects under way, the most visible will be SOM's Jin Mao Building to be built for the China Shanghai Foreign Trade Centre, which is part of the Ministry of Foreign Trade and Economic Development, and due to be completed in 1998. A 558-room Hyatt Hotel is slated to be included in this 265,000 m² tower. The choice of SOM, who won a 1993 competition for the project, is undoubtedly related to the large size of this Chicago and New York based partnership, founded in 1936. Having built in forty countries, such a firm is well suited to deal with the inherent complexities of building in such a new environment. Efficient, making widespread use of computer-aided design, SOM may not have created an innovative design here, but the point, it seems, is to go high fast.

Another SOM project, although unlikely to be built, is even more spectacular than the Jin Mao Building. The so-called Russia Tower in Moscow would be no less than 126 stories high. SOM's own press release acknowledges the highly symbolic nature of such a design: "The celebration of the tall object, of the ability to build skyward, has been of symbolic importance throughout history. The vertical has always been considered the 'sacred' dimension of space. It represents a path towards a higher reality, a reality which conquers gravity, transcends earthly existence, and ensures communication with the sky." Usually considered an expression of raw economic power, the tower is here transformed into a quasi-religious object, an interesting transition from the days of the Stalinist skyscrapers that still dot Moscow. There may yet be a way to find the "Workers' Paradise."

Skidmore, Owings & Merrill's description of the merits of the Russia Tower has the advantage of being honest about the charged symbolic content of the tall building, which has never really been considered a very positive contribution to the difficulties of urban congestion. Although Hiroshi Hara's dream of an "electronic city" may still seem a bit far-fetched, his Umeda Sky City, standing out starkly against the mostly low-rise buildings of Osaka, has an undeniable urban presence and an inventive form. Contemporary expressions of the age-old drive toward monumental architecture, the other towers presented here may indeed serve an inspirational role for some, even if the "sacred" dimension suggested in the case of the Russia Tower is still out of their reach.

Pages 68/69
**HLW International
Chongqing Office Tower
Chongqing, Sichuan, China,
1995 (project)**
Commissioned by Chongqing
National Garden City, Inc. as a
mixed-use commercial office
and hotel, this tower would be
located in downtown Chongqing,
just west of the juncture of the
Yangtze and Jialing Rivers.
The 50 year lease for the land
requires that the structure be
a minimum of 100 stories tall,
reaching 516 m at the tip of
its antenna.

Skidmore, Owings & Merrill
Russia Tower
Moscow, Russia, 1992 (project)
Although it is quite unlikely that this building will in fact be built, it would have featured no less than 126 stories, with offices, a hotel, retail space and parking for 600 cars. It is described by the architects as "a symbol of communication between Russia and the modern world."

Skidmore, Owings & Merrill
Jin Mao Building
Shanghai, China, 1994 (project)
This tower, projected for the Pudong development district of Shanghai, would be eighty-eight stories and 419 m tall. Offices would be located on the first fifty floors and a Grand Hyatt Hotel with an atrium no less than thirty-one stories high on the upper floors.

Temporary Structures

An emphasis on the problems of urban design, inevitable in a period when the decay of old cities and the rise of new centers is a defining phenomenon throughout the world, brings with it the question of what can be considered "permanent" in contemporary architecture. Certain structures, like I.M. Pei's Louvre pyramid, or Ben van Berkel's new Erasmus Bridge in Rotterdam, are clearly intended to be as long-lasting as possible. The techniques of modern architecture certainly equip it to be able to deal with such circumstances, but more frequently the shape of the modern city changes as a very high pace. A boutique, even one designed by a famous architect, may not last more than two or three years. A building may be swept away in less than a decade by the pace of urban renewal and expansion. Surprisingly enough, outstanding examples of temporary architecture are relatively rare, and yet it is clear that a demand exists for inexpensive structures, destined only to last a few years.

New Yorker Steven Holl (born in 1947) has achieved a substantial degree of international recognition with projects that challenge assumptions about architectural space, light and durability. His Storefront for Art and Architecture, a collaborative project located in Manhattan, which he conceived with the artist Vito Acconci, is a radical design that has neither windows nor doors in the traditional sense of the words. Rather this is an adaptive response to the "nomadic" conditions of contemporary urban life, accomplished with a very limited budget, and destined to be replaced with a new design very quickly.

Steven Holl
Storefront for Art
and Architecture
New York, New York, 1994
Located at the eastern boundary of the Soho area of downtown New York, this highly unusual gallery was designed by the architect in collaboration with the artist Vito Acconci. As sculptural as it is truly practical, the design was intended to be used only for a relatively short period of time before another architect would be called on to redo the space.

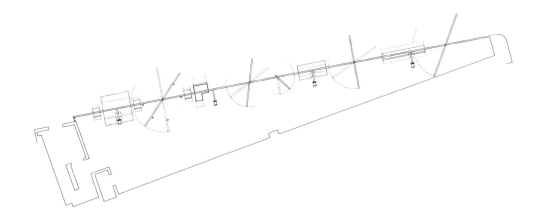

Pages 72/73
Steven Holl
Storefront for Art
and Architecture
New York, New York, 1994
The entire facade of the Storefront pivots either vertically or
horizontally, providing direct
access to the street. The interior
of the narrow, triangular space is
finished in a minimal way, providing the necessary space for architectural, urban or artistic presen-
tations, which usually carry a
political message.

Pages 74/75
Hodgetts + Fung
Towell Temporary Library, UCLA
Los Angeles, California, 1991–93
Erected in the midst of UCLA's
Brentwood campus as a replacement facility for the Powell
Library during the "seismic
upgrading" of that structure,
this temporary structure shows
the extent to which ephemeral
buildings can be attractive,
functional and economical.

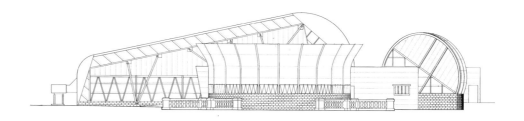

Holl is one of the more thoughtful contemporary architects. He has written, "As in Ovid's *Metamorphoses*, 'Knowledge of the world means dissolving the solidity of the world.'" So in the paradigm shifts of today all material heaviness seems to disappear. The devices propelling this world of information flow utilize non-material impulses in a visual field. Computer-aided design, motion control, virtual reality, magnetic resonance imaging, computer animation, synthetic holography – to name a few of the present means – are all rapidly developing vectors of information, which are characterized by motion and light.

"The horror of current events is projected into domestic living rooms everywhere. Likewise, a soulless fashionable commercialism characterizes many of the arts. As we allow ourselves to be victims of unconscious habits, skipping from gesture to final image, we leap over the simmering of feelings and thoughts that carries a slow-developing intensity of ideas and forms and their interior spatial consequences.

An architecture fusing these worlds of flow and difference is inconsistent by nature. As the differences of individual circumstance are essential, this architecture must accept Emerson's admonition, 'Consistency is the hobgoblin of little minds.' Rather than conforming to technological or stylistic uniformity, this architecture would be open to the irrationalities of place. It would resist the homogenizing tendencies of standardization ... A new architecture must be formed that is simultaneously aligned with transcultural continuity and with the poetic expression of individual situations and communities."[15]

Pages 76/77
Schneider + Schumacher
Info Box
Berlin, Germany, 1995
Set up above the ground as though to emphasize its temporary nature, the Info Box is also highly visible because of its color and its situation in the midst of the Potsdamer Platz construction area. It calls, on the one hand, on a vocabulary related to shipping containers, and on another level brings to mind some contemporary sculpture.

In different circumstances, other American architects, Hodgetts + Fung have evolved toward a different approach to the essentially nomadic nature of much contemporary design. Their Towell Library (1991–93), situated in the midst of UCLA's Brentwood campus, was intended as a temporary replacement for Powell Library, the main undergraduate facility, which was to undergo a three to five year closure for seismic renovation. According to the architects, "the complex consists of four linked tented forms conceived to look different and unpredictable from all directions." Using a white and gold polyester skin, cinder block walls, off-the-shelf lighting, or exposed sprinkler pipes, the architects succeeding in completing the building, which receives 500 students at a time, for the low, budget price of $3.5 million. Known for their projects related to the entertainment industry, Craig Hodgetts and Ming Fung, who have taught at SCI-Arc since 1987, encouraged the idea with this building that informal, low-cost temporary structures can also be well designed, a concept that is of interest, for example, to the city of Los Angeles because of its large homeless population. Berlin, the once and future capital of a reunited Germany, presents another face of urban change. In the Mitte area alone, some 900 construction projects are in various stages of planning, with the Federal Chancellery, Tiergarten tunnel and new central Lehrter Bahnhof all already under construction. This station, designed by Von Gerkan, Marg and Partner, will boast a

400 m long trussed-glass hall. In the area of the Potsdamer Platz, where Mercedes-Benz, Sony and others have planned a city-within-the city (an expression that might bring to mind the ambitious plans of Kuala Lumpur or Shanghai), the architects Schneider + Schumacher have erected a temporary structure called the Info Box, intended to give residents information on the massive transformation that their city is undergoing. Because it is situated on a future work site, the Info Box will inevitably disappear, but its cantilevered, metallic structure announces that it has no pretensions to permanence, much as the Towell Temporary Library seems also to be ephemeral by nature.

Ephemeral architecture is of course an inevitable part of urban expansion, but when they are successful, such buildings often have a longer life than was originally intended. It will be recalled that the Eiffel Tower was to be no more than a grandiose modern symbol for the 1889 Universal Exhibition in Paris. Such fairs have generated a great deal of temporary architecture, and continue to do so in spite of their perilous economic equilibrium. A recent example is the Seville Expo '92, which led to the construction of a new airport terminal by Rafael Moneo, and bridges by the likes of Santiago Calatrava. Within the fair grounds on the Cartuja island, Tadao Ando's monumental wooden Japanese pavilion stands out as an unusually audacious design. Like a great ark overlooking the Guadalquivir River and the neighboring countryside, it solved many of the problems inherent in temporary designs, while showing the Japanese affinity for wood. All of this from an architect best known for his very solid concrete structures.

The pressure to provide lodging and commercial space in modern cities, and the need to be able to convert existing buildings to other uses, all plead in favor of an increasing use of inexpensive materials and intentionally ephemeral designs. It is the task of quality architects too to provide this sort of facility, which in many ways may mark the visitor's mind and spirit more than many allegedly permanent buildings.

Pages 78/79
Tadao Ando
Japanese Pavilion, Expo '92
Seville, Spain, 1992
Although exhibition pavilions are usually by definition ephemeral, Tadao Ando took advantage of the 1992 Seville exhibition to carry out his largest-scale experiment in the use of wood, a typical Japanese material, but not one he usually favors.

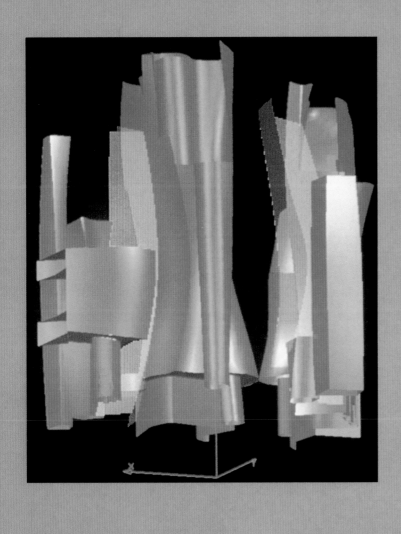

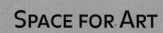

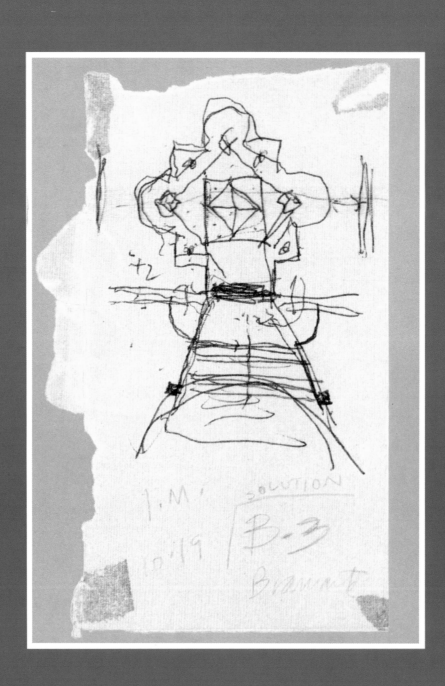

A new Generation of Museums

Page 81
Frank O. Gehry
Guggenheim Museum
Bilbao, Spain, 1991–97
Through the extensive use of
computer assisted design, and
in particular the CATIA program
developed by Dassault for fighter
plane design, Gehry has managed
to give highly unusual forms to
his new museum in Bilbao.

Page 82
I.M. Pei
Grand Louvre
Paris, France, 1982–94
An early original sketch by I.M. Pei
for the Louvre pyramid and the
basins that surround it recall that
he was inspired in part by the
garden designs of Le Nôtre, who
made use of the abstract presence
of sky and water. Pei's design of
course evolved before the completion of the pyramid itself in 1989.

Europe Leads the Way

Throughout the 1980s, and into the early 1990s, a wave of museum construction
swept across Europe, and certainly concerned Japan, if only to a lesser degree the
United States. The reasoning behind this trend is relatively clear. Whereas the great
cathedrals of the past may have been potent symbols of the wealth or importance
of European cities, culture seems to have replaced religion as the most obvious sign
of success. France, under François Mitterrand, engaged in an unparalleled series of
cultural projects, known as the *Grands Travaux*. The most visible, and perhaps the
most significant of these efforts was undoubtedly the Louvre Pyramid designed by
the Chinese-born American architect I.M. Pei. Born in 1917 in Canton, Pei was called
on directly by President Mitterrand, without any prior competition, to redesign the
"greatest museum in the world." More than a central entrance, the Louvre project
entailed the development of a master-plan for the expansion of the museum into
the vast areas of the Richelieu Wing, long occupied by France's Ministry of Finance.
Quite obviously, a royal palace such as the Louvre is not the ideal location for a museum of art, if only because of its U-shaped layout, requiring long walks between
the different wings. This fact led I.M. Pei to conclude that the only possible location
for the new entrance would have to be at the center of the structure. Long used as
a parking lot, the so-called Cour Napoleon became the heart of the Grand Louvre.
In its first phase, completed in 1989, the Grand Louvre project entailed the erection
of the now famous pyramid, but also the construction of large underground areas to
accommodate the facilities such as shops, restaurants and auditoriums, which were
sorely lacking until that time. Although politically oriented protests greeted the an-
nouncement of the project, the French public came to accept the pyramid as the
newest of a long line of great Parisian landmarks. Criticized in particular for his lack
of apparent sympathy for the surrounding nineteenth century architecture, Pei
explained that the pyramid design was in fact deeply rooted in French tradition.
Citing his personal admiration for the garden designer Le Nôtre, responsible for the
nearby Tuileries gardens, Pei pointed out that two essential elements of Le Nôtre's
garden designs had in fact been sky and water. With the basins ringing the pyramid,
and its own reflective surface showing the image of passing clouds, the new addition was in reality a subtle blend of geometric modernity and tradition.

Perhaps because of his background as an able designer of commercial projects in
the earlier part of his career, Pei has never been as fully accepted by the American
architectural establishment as his achievements would warrant. Few in the United
States seem to have fully understood the extent to which the Grand Louvre project,
with its second Richelieu Wing phase completed in 1993, represents one of the
greatest architectural accomplishments of the late twentieth century. Not only did
I.M. Pei succeed here in giving appropriate form to François Mitterrand's ambition
to place culture at the heart of France's political agenda, but he also mastered the
extremely delicate equilibrium that had to be obtained between the symbolic
weight of a great historical monument and the requirements of the modern age. The

bold simplicity of Pei's pyramid places it at once in the tradition of modern architecture and shows how it is possible to shed a new light on the buildings of centuries past. As President Mitterrand said during an inaugural speech for the pyramid, the former Cour Napoleon parking area was nothing more than a dangerous place to go at night, whereas after the intervention of I.M. Pei, it added a great new square to central Paris, no small accomplishment in itself.

The success of certain Paris cultural projects undoubtedly encouraged some provincial French cities to do likewise. Foremost amongst these was the southern city of Nîmes, known for its well-preserved Roman monuments. Here, in one of the most prestigious sites available, just opposite the Roman temple, the Maison Carrée, mayor Jean Bousquet decided to erect a modern temple to culture. In a 1984 competition, he called on the cream of contemporary architects – Sir Norman Foster, Frank O. Gehry, Hans Hollein, Arata Isozaki, Richard Meier, Jean Nouvel, Aldo Rossi, Alvaro Siza and James Stirling – to study the project. Chosen at that time, Sir Norman Foster completed the Carré d'Art only in 1993, with delays resulting most notably from severe flooding of the city center. In an even more obvious way than the Louvre pyramid, the Carré d'Art represents a classical solution to the

Pages 84/85
I.M. Pei
Louvre Pyramid
Paris, France, 1982–89
Called on to make the Louvre Palace a modern museum by French president François Mitterrand, Pei settled to the solution of the centrally located pyramid, with a spectacular underground entrance hall, which includes the spiral staircase visible in the image to the left. Three smaller pyramids provide light in the underground areas.

delicate problem of the insertion of modern architecture into an historical urban environment. A far cry from the early Modernist tendency to ignore surrounding architecture, the Carré d'Art shows just how well a subtly "high tech" building can face and respond to the classical Roman order of the Maison Carrée. At the date of the conception of the Carré d'Art, this achievement is not related either to the later concern for extreme economy in construction, or to the full use of computer technology. Rather, it is evidence of the coming to maturity, not only of Sir Norman Foster, but also of modern architecture in general. Challenged by the emergence of the Post-Modern style to once again seek integration into the urban environment, as opposed to the rejection that typified much earlier work, architects who continued to work with the clean lines of the modern demonstrated here and elsewhere that contemporary buildings could be infused with a kind of classicism, which by no means required the use of pastiche.

The state-led cultural projects of France were not necessarily imitated elsewhere in Europe, but for similar reasons cultural projects have been privileged. For the

California architect Frank O. Gehry this trend has been a source of some of his most successful and large-scale projects. The Vitra Design Museum, located in Weil am Rhein, Germany, just across the border from Basel, Switzerland, is a case in point. Here, a large manufacturer of office furniture decided that calling on "name" architects made good business sense. For their large holding of museum quality chairs, Vitra asked Frank O. Gehry to create an unusual space, a challenge that he met in a brilliant fashion. Though not very large, the Vitra Museum is full of unexpected, soaring spaces, which are far from the accepted norms of modern architecture. Rather, this is a sculptural environment, which succeeds in giving a place of honor to the exhibited furniture while existing in its own right as a work of art.

Gehry's sense of sculptural forms is being carried to new heights in the Bilbao Museum, under construction in Bilbao, Spain. Here, a sophisticated computer program known as CATIA, used by the French plane manufacturer Dassault to design the curves of fighter planes, has been harnessed to permit the creation of unusually elaborate shapes. Because of the flexibility of the computer-aided design process, both working models and final production drawings can be matched to a manufacturing process that makes it possible to control costs while creating unique forms. Despite his artistic temperament, Gehry's importance lies here in his capacity to make technology do his bidding while solving the practical problems of construction.

Germany and The Netherlands have of course shown the way in Europe with the construction of numerous new museums. Hans Hollein's Frankfurt Museum of Modern Art is a case in point. On a difficult, triangular site in Frankfurt, he created a sort of modern version of the steamship design often seen in early twentieth century architecture. Although it does hearken back to the Post-Modern esthetic of the 1970s, the Frankfurt Museum's complex spaces and imposing presence make it one of the cultural landmarks of Germany.

Certainly less severe and more unexpected, Alessandro Mendini's Groninger Museum in Groningen, The Netherlands, is an ode to the joy of design and color. The new museum, built by the municipality of this northern Dutch city with a generous donation from the local Netherlands Gasunie company, is situated on an artificial island on a canal near the central railroad station. A bridge crossing through the middle of the museum is the most direct route from the station to the city center for at least two million people per year, so a large number of casual visitors are almost guaranteed for the institution. Mendini is of course best known for his vibrantly colored furniture designs. Here, he conceived of a complex that has been likened to the Egyptian temple of Philae, calling on a number of other architects and designers, including the Frenchman Philippe Starck. Despite the different approaches of each designer, the impression given by the whole of this museum is one of joyous celebration, a rare enough event, especially in the often sanctimonious museum world. As Mendini says, "I think that a museum nowadays has a similar role to that of the church in past centuries. It is a place for relaxation with respect to the rapid passage of time —This also coincides with the intention to free museums, at last, from the rhetoric and the elitist paternalism of art." Both the Groninger's director Frans Haks

Pages 86/87
Sir Norman Foster
Carré d'Art
Nîmes, France, 1985–93
It was the former mayor of Nîmes, Jean Bousquet, who is also the President of the Cacharel clothing company, who instigated the 1984 competition that selected Sir Norman Foster to design a new "médiathèque" on a highly visible and historically sensitive site facing the temple known as the Maison Carrée, which was built c. 12 B.C.

and Mendini clearly believe that fewer distinctions should be made between the visual arts, design and architecture, and their efforts are intended to prove the viability of a complete symbiosis. Raucous in its debauchery of colors and forms, the Groninger Museum is nonetheless resolutely connected to the city and to the history of architecture, reaching back to Egypt and forward to the surprisingly disjointed pavilion by Coop Himmelblau – this despite Mendini's self-proclaimed effort to create internal spaces that "alienate" the visitor, and despite the building's apparent connection to design styles that had their heyday in the 1980s if not before. It should be pointed out that the flamboyant architecture of Mendini *et al.* does not correspond to a very significant art collection. The inaugural show, dedicated to none other than Mendini himself, highlighted the significant holdings of the institution in Memphis-type furniture, but did little to allay the suspicion that there were more "smoke and mirrors" here than great art. Architecture and design seem to be at the center of this effort, which is in itself a positive observation.

Apparently less given to joyous excess, the Swiss architects Herzog & de Meuron were selected in April 1994 to design the new Tate Gallery of Modern Art in London's abandoned Bankside Power Station, just across the Thames from St Paul's Cathedral. Destined to contain at least 12,000 m² of gallery space, this new project will be financed partially through the UK's Millennium Fund. On October 30, 1995, it was announced by the Millennium Commission that a grant of no less than £50 million had been awarded to the Tate for the Bankside rehabilitation. Located near the new Globe Theater, it is hoped that the Tate Gallery of Modern Art will permit the regeneration of an entire new quarter of London. It is estimated that the project, whose total cost will be £106 million, "will create 650 jobs locally and 2,400 throughout London, generating approximately £50 million in additional economic activity each year in an area with very high levels of unemployment." Aside from any esthetic considerations related to the architectural plan, this description, contained in a Tate Gallery press release, demonstrates the great attention given to the economic impact of any publicly funded cultural project. Costs and benefits are much more carefully studied now than in the past, and architects are bound to take this into consideration. Herzog & de Meuron were chosen over a stellar field of competitors, including David Chipperfield, Tadao Ando, Renzo Piano, Rafael Moneo and Rem Koolhaas, proving if need be the continued attraction of the well-known names of architecture for such important museum designs. Although the final scheme will emerge only after long work between the architects and the curators, it is clear that the new Tate Gallery for Modern Art will be an ode to strict simplicity, centered around a stripped-down 150 m long turbine hall. It is interesting to note that Jacques Herzog has declared, "I support the idea of the architect as artist, but I think that to apply the image of art to architecture is the worst thing you can do. Contemporary architecture tends to behave like an advertising copywriter; it exploits the field of art, taking advantage of art in order to renew its own image

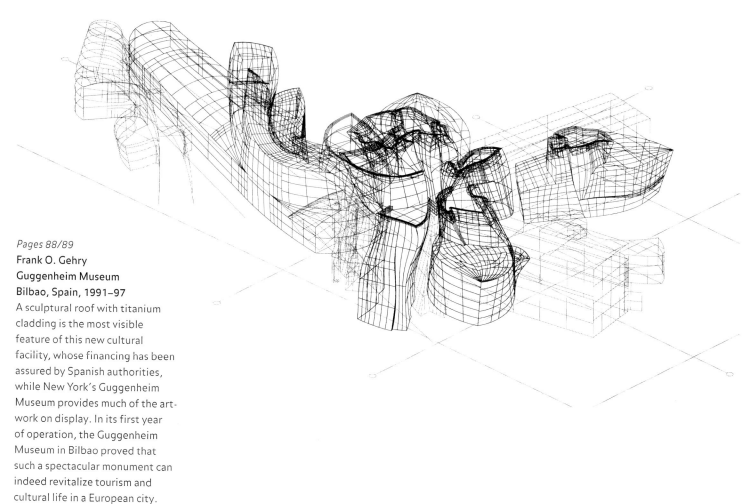

Pages 88/89
Frank O. Gehry
Guggenheim Museum
Bilbao, Spain, 1991–97
A sculptural roof with titanium
cladding is the most visible
feature of this new cultural
facility, whose financing has been
assured by Spanish authorities,
while New York's Guggenheim
Museum provides much of the art-
work on display. In its first year
of operation, the Guggenheim
Museum in Bilbao proved that
such a spectacular monument can
indeed revitalize tourism and
cultural life in a European city.

Pages 90/91
Hans Hollein
Frankfurt Museum of Modern Art
Frankfurt/Main, Germany,
1982–90
Located on a difficult triangular
site, which confers a boat-like image on the building, the Frankfurt
Museum of Modern Art is further
proof of this city's commitment to
the arts, although Hollein's structure has been accused of being
rather heavy. Other Frankfurt cultural institutions, mostly located
on the Museumsufer, include the
Museum of Decorative Arts by
Richard Meier and the nearby
Architecture Museum by Oswald
Matthias Ungers. To the left, a
work by the French artist Christian
Boltanski in the museum.

without reflecting its conceptual foundations – and everybody gets tired of applied images. To escape being trapped in the world of Post-Modern graphics, the architect can also over-react by finding himself converted into a pure pragmatist." The radical simplicity of Herzog & de Meuron is thus their own argument for the renewed status of the architect, not as "advertising copywriter" but as Artist, with a capital A.

As in numerous other instances, contemporary architecture is being brought to bear in the Bankside Power Station on the problem of existing industrial structures, rather than totally new construction. This is an important trend in recent design, and serves the cause of bringing patrimonial architecture into a much closer dialogue with the modern world. Simply stated, the quality of older buildings is often such that it is much less expensive to refit the interiors than to demolish and build anew. Architects are now obliged to confront and assimilate this heritage, whereas they often rejected it in the past.

Japan's Thirst for Art

The economic "miracle" of Japan, although dulled by the recession and real estate debacle of the early 1990s, gave rise to a formidable thirst for culture. Japan naturally had its share of museums of traditional art, although the country never had a coherent national museum policy. Even today the limited number of national museums receive low levels of financing from the government. Rather it is the prefectoral, municipal and private museums that have sprung up across the country that have rightly given Japan the reputation as being one of the most active countries in terms of the creation of these institutions. The point of creating a museum in Japan, even more than in other countries, is to symbolically announce the wealth or success of a city or company. For this reason, the new museums are often little more than empty shells, but the shells tend to be grandiose. What better solution in such instances than to call on famous architects to create spectacular buildings? The problem of the formation of the collections is often left in limbo, all the more so because Japan does not really have a system for the proper university-level formation of curators. Curators and museum directors, with some notable exceptions, are more likely to be administrators than persons who have a real passion for art. All of this said, the Japanese taste for innovative architecture, and the quality of construction, have meant that several new institutions are housed in truly remarkable buildings.

Tadao Ando, for example, the Osaka-based master of concrete architecture, recently built the Naoshima Museum of Contemporary Art on an isolated island in the Inland Sea. Situated on a hilltop overlooking the heavily traveled waterways

Herzog & de Meuron
Tate Gallery of Modern Art
Bankside Power Station
London, Great Britain, 1995–2000
Situated just opposite St Paul's Cathedral on the Thames, the new Tate Gallery facility in the former Bankside Power Station building will take advantage of the existing space, and in particular the enormous turbine hall, to exhibit the holdings of the Tate in British and foreign modern art, with the basic collections of English art remaining in the older Millbank buildings.

Tadao Ando
Naoshima Museum and Hotel
Naoshima, Kagawa, Japan,
Phase I, 1990–92
Located on a relatively unspoiled
island in the Inland Sea of Japan,
this combined hotel and museum
of contemporary art calls on the
architect's acute sense of topography. By digging into the site,
Tadao Ando has created something akin to an earthwork. As he
says, "There is a plan to have me
design one building a year all over
this area. Every time you go, there
will be something under construction. This will be kept up for ten,
twenty years. This project in
its conception is very much like
contemporary art."

between Shikoku and Honshu, this striking complex includes a luxurious hotel. As
unexpected as the museum/hotel combination may seem, it is important to know in
this instance that new construction is severely restricted on an island like Naoshima,
unless the project involves a cultural component. Despite a number of interesting
works of contemporary art, and a perfectly viable exhibition space, the Naoshima
Museum of Contemporary Art is in some sense an excuse for the hotel operation.

Two museums created by Toyo Ito are less subjected to disguised commercial objectives. His Yatsushiro Municipal Museum, in Yatsushiro on the southern island of
Kyushu, is an exemplary illustration of Ito's capacity to create a light, seemingly almost wind-borne architecture. This otherwise relatively depressing industrial city,
located just a few kilometers from Minimata where W. Eugene Smith's wrenching
portraits of the victims of mercury poisoning were taken in the 1970s, is given a
more clearly defined cultural identity by a museum whose purpose is to highlight
local history. Set on an artificial hill, the Yatsushiro Museum is one of the most
striking architectural forms to emerge from Japan in recent years. Another Ito structure is his Shimosuwa Lake Suwa Museum, located in central Honshu, the heart of
Japan. As mentioned above, the very shape of this museum is an indication that
new, more sculptural forms are emerging in contemporary architecture.

Arata Isozaki's small Nagi MoCA, located in the Okayama Prefecture, carries a
more ambitious agenda for museum architecture in its own eccentric forms.
According to this Tokyo-based architect, there have been two generations in museum architecture. The first is exemplified by the use of historical buildings, as in

the Louvre. The second generation is illustrated by more flexible modern institutions such as the Pompidou Center and the Museum of Modern Art in New York. Now, says Isozaki, the time is ripe for a third generation that abandons the conventional concept of a museum and provides specially designed spaces and settings for newly created and installed art. The town of Nagi counts only 7,500 inhabitants and as such could not be expected to boast a substantial art collection. So here, Isozaki not only conceived the architecture, but provided the art as well, with site-specific installations designed by his wife, the sculptor Aiko Miyawaki, Shusaku Arakawa and Kazuo Okazaki. Further, the museum and art design is integrated into a symbolic triad formed by the sun, moon and earth, the whole aligned with a nearby "sacred" mountain. The Nagi MoCA is of importance not because of its size but because of its integrated effort to create a symbolic structure, in harmony both with the art that it houses and gives significance to, and with the local traditions and topography. Its rather blocky forms do not have the lyrical grace of Ito's light architecture, but Isozaki's thinking here has clearly gone beyond one of attractive shapes.

A final example, which may not be the most successful work by Fumihiko Maki, is the Kyoto Museum of Modern Art, situated near the Okazaki park in the northwestern section of the city, just next to the enormous red torii of the Heian Temple. Its large rectilinear bulk stands out, and its rather awkward white entrance area

Toyo Ito
Yatsushiro Municipal Museum
Yatsushiro, Kumamoto, Japan, 1989–91
Located on an artificial hill, this museum of local history is the first of three buildings in the otherwise rather unremarkable Kyushu town of Yatsushiro, by Ito. He also designed the Elderly People's Home (1992–94) and a Fire Station (1992–95).

Arata Isozaki
Nagi MoCA
Nagi-cho, Okayama, Japan,
1992–94
This small museum was designed
by Isozaki for the permanent
display of the works of three
contemporary Japanese artists. In
this image, the work by Shusaku
Arakawa, which represents mirror
images of the famous Kyoto
garden of Ryoan-ji, is situated
in an inclined tube (see page 96),
which makes it very difficult for
the viewer to stand up straight.

seems to accentuate the fundamentally weak holdings displayed within. This is one
of Japan's few national museums, with limited funding provided by the Japanese
Ministry of Finance. Because of administrative wrangling, it took no less than
sixteen years to go from the original project designed by Maki in 1970 to the 1986
opening. Created in 1963 as an annex of the Tokyo Museum of Modern Art, the
Kyoto Museum did not have a single work of modern art of its own at that date,
which explains a good deal of the current emptiness. The rest is undoubtedly
explained by the fact that the acquisitions budget, of less than one million dollars a
year, has not been increased in more than ten years. Because Japan has no fiscal
encouragement for donations to national museums, the Kyoto National Museum of
Modern Art is left to fend for itself, seeking as it may to fill the large modern spaces
designed by Fumihiko Maki.

Pages 96/97
Arata Isozaki
Nagi MoCA
Nagi-cho, Okayama, Japan,
1992–94
Near the entrance area of the Nagi
Museum of Contemporary Art,
this rather successful work by Aiko
Miyawaki symbolizing the earth is
placed in the axis of the nearby
"sacred mountain" Nagi-san.
A reflecting pool amplifies the
effect of the gently swaying
stainless steel wire sculpture.

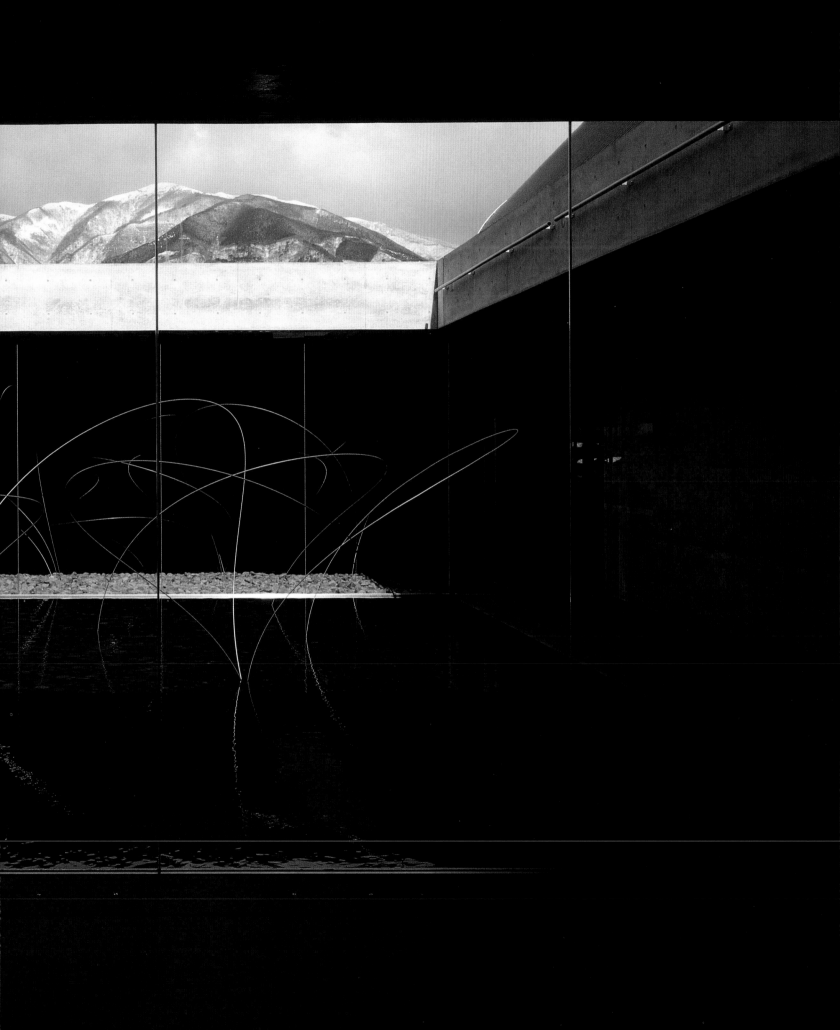

Fumihiko Maki
National Museum of Modern Art
Kyoto, Japan, 1983–86
Fumihiko Maki completed his first
design for this new museum in
1970, located in the Okazaki Park
in the northeastern part of Kyoto.
It is directly next to an enormous
red torii, which marks the
entrance to the Heian Temple.
Zoning in this historic area limited
the building to a 20 m height.
The museum, which has a limited
collection, receives between
400,000 and 500,000 visitors a
year.

Mario Botta
San Francisco Museum
of Modern Art
San Francisco, California, 1990–94
In this image, Fumihiko Maki's
Yerba Buena Center is visible in
the foreground, and one of the
towers of the Bay Bridge in the
background. With its massive
brick veneer volume, Botta's
museum does not appear to be
directly related to any of the
surrounding architecture. It does,
however, confer a sense of the importance that both the architect
and the museum trustees wished
to give to the art they display
within its walls.

New American Homes for Culture

The American system has permitted the creation of numerous museums, despite
an almost total lack of government support. The direct intervention by central
governments favored in Europe, for example, is of course replaced by the fiscal
encouragement of donations in the United States. Because of the recession that
marked the later part of the 1980s, the creation of new museums in the United
States certainly slowed, although the West and Southwest continued to feel a need
to develop their cultural resources more than the developed East.

One of the most ambitious museum projects in the United States to be completed in recent years is Mario Botta's San Francisco Museum of Modern Art (1990–
94). There was no competition as such held for the choice of the architect of this centrally located 18,500 m² museum. Rather, the Trustees of the Museum, which was
created in 1935, interviewed five architects: Mario Botta, Frank O. Gehry, Thomas
Beeby, Tadao Ando, and Charles Moore. Located on Third Street, near the Moscone
Convention Center, the museum, which opened on January 18, 1995, is part of an
urban redevelopment program covering an area of more than 40 hectares, first
envisaged by the city of San Francisco in 1954. It is located across the street from
Fumihiko Maki's new Yerba Buena Center, whose light, ship-like style seems at odds
with Botta's brick veneer cladding, and massive, almost windowless design. A central *oculus*, which appears on the exterior of the building in the form of a truncated
cylinder, brings light to the five stories of the building, and particularly to the
generous, 7 m high top-lit galleries on the upper floor. Built on city land put at the
disposition of SFMoMA by the redevelopment agency responsible for the Yerba
Buena district, the new structure was built at a cost of $60 million, provided almost
entirely by private donations.

The wealth of the San Francisco Museum of Modern Art, like that of other similar institutions across the United States, naturally depends on the formation of major private collections, which eventually find their way into the public domain. Southern California, with its film and electronics industries, has been an area where the collection of contemporary art, for example, has recently become quite fashionable. Of course few clients have the means to build a private museum of their own, but Frank Israel's Art Pavilion, located in Beverly Hills (1991), is an outstanding example of what can happen in the United States when a talented architect and a major collector join forces. Located in an exclusive residential area, this 1,100 m² freestanding pavilion is next to the large home of the client, and connected to it by an underground passage. Intended to house his art collection and two floors of studio space, the structure is likened by the architect to a "great ark, containing an important collection of abstract expressionist art, yet empowered by its contents to become a piece of art in the terraced sculpture garden." The most spectacular space is undoubtedly the 8.5 m high top floor with its large timber trusses. The materials used are fiberglass-reinforced concrete for the upper, outside walls, with stucco below, chosen to create a harmony with the original house. The roof is covered in sheet metal and tile. A surprising exterior feature is a protruding boat-shaped balcony. As the architect says, "A smaller version of the great ark, it is intended to appear as if it were being raised from the garden below." Frank Israel's reference to this building as a "piece of art" is one that should be retained, because it is yet another bit of evidence of the strengthened links between the visual arts and architecture.

Rarely are art and architecture so intimately related, though, as in the Storefront for Art and Architecture designed by Steven Holl and the artist Vito Acconci in New York. Located on Kenmare Street, at the eastern extremity of the Soho gallery area in Manhattan, this tiny wedge-shaped space stands out at once because it does not have windows in any traditional sense of the word. Rather, pivoting concrete-and-wood fiber panels replace the old storefront. Cut into differently sized geometric shapes, the panels open completely toward the street, with the interior of the space being left much as it was, aside from a small office cubicle. The Storefront is a well-known New York location for rather politically oriented exhibitions, and the director of the space, Kyong Park, hopes to commission a redesign of the gallery every two years. Although this may not in fact be the immediate fate of Steven Holl's design, the point that much contemporary architecture and design is fundamentally ephemeral has been made. The Pace Collection Showroom designed by Holl at the corner of 72nd Street and Madison Avenue (1985–86), for example, has already been replaced by a Ralph Lauren clothing store. The Storefront, where art meets architecture, is radical design for a new, unsettled era.

The significant development of art museums in the United States over the decades following World War II may in fact have reached a plateau. There are, after all, only so many masterpieces to be found, and with so many other museums around the world competing for them, it may no longer be very reasonable to expect to be able to fill new galleries, unless an institution has the means of the Getty Trust. A new trend in culturally oriented architecture both in the United States and elsewhere is certainly toward museums that are oriented to history, society or to the performing arts. A significant example of such an institution in the United States is James Freed's Holocaust Memorial in Washington, D.C.

Freed's former partner, I.M. Pei, completed the somewhat controversial Rock and Roll Hall of Fame in Cleveland, Ohio, in 1995. Pei may not have been the obvious choice to build a monument to Rock and Roll, and he did receive a fair amount of criticism. As he candidly says, "I prefer jazz," but the 14,000 m² facility that he designed on the shores of Lake Erie is a tribute to the idea of architecture as "frozen music." As the music in this case is exuberant or even violent at times, Pei's surpris-

Page 101
Mario Botta
San Francisco Museum
of Modern Art
San Francisco, California, 1990–94
The central oculus of the SFMoMA building brings a considerable amount of light not only into the upper gallery levels, but down into the entrance area five floors below. This truncated cone form is rather typical of Botta's architecture, having been used for example in a different manner in his Évry Cathedral in France.

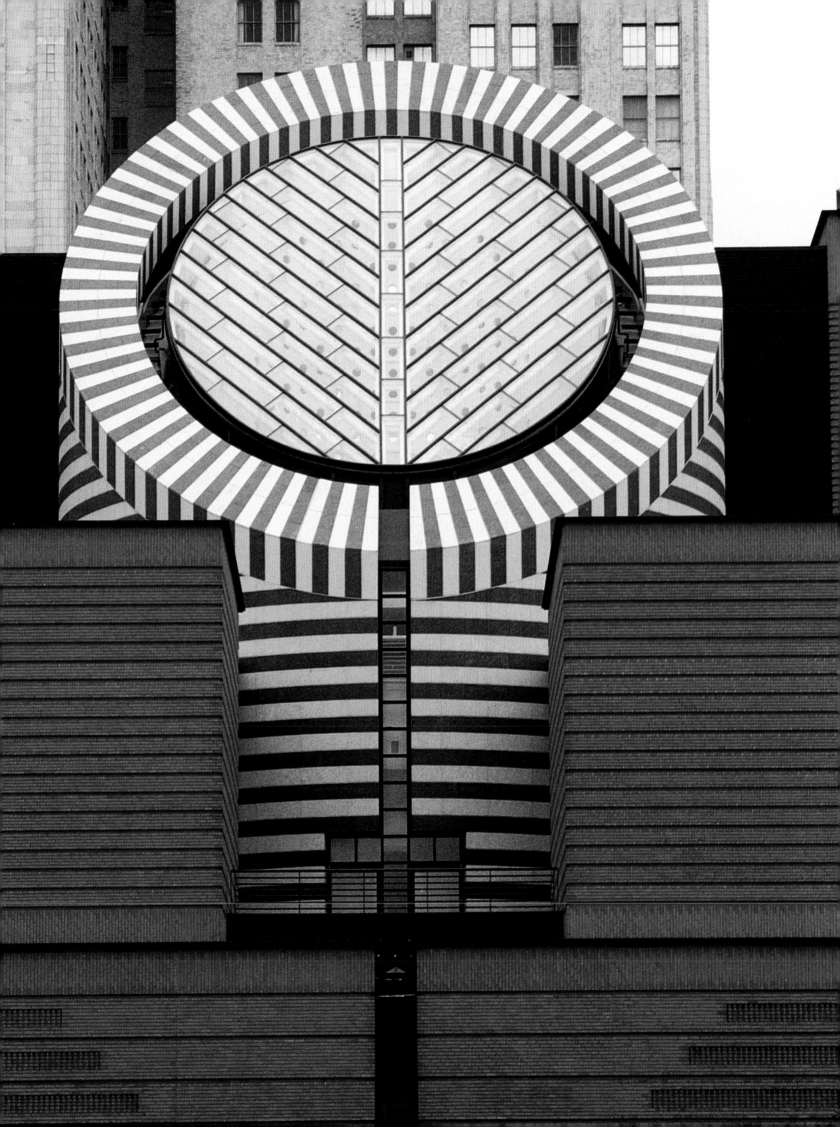

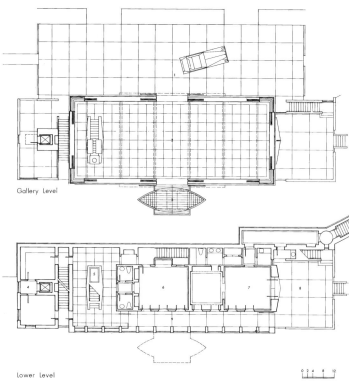

Gallery Level

Lower Level

0 2 4   8   12

Pages 102/103
Franklin Israel
Art Pavilion
Beverly Hills, California, 1991
This is a freestanding pavilion situated next to a large hillside home in Los Angeles. There is a gallery for the art collection of the client and two floors of studio and related space. One of its most striking features is a large boat-shaped balcony, which the architect called "a smaller version of the great ark." Israel, one of the most talented California architects of the post-Gehry generation, died in 1996.

ing, cantilevered asymmetrical volumes are too. The most evident features of the building are a 50 m high concrete tower, which serves in part to support a 35 m high triangular glass "tent" housing the spectacular entrance volume. Inclined at a 45° angle, this glazed surface recalls numerous other Pei buildings, including the Louvre Pyramid. In an unusual configuration, some 3,000 m² of exhibition space are situated underground, beneath the public plaza, whereas the two cantilevered volumes, a trapezoid and a drum respectively, contain a 125-seat theater and a dance area (still to be installed). A third floor café gives a view of the entrance volume, and the actual hall of fame is at the top of the tower in a space described by the "New York Times" as "lugubrious." Aside from defining the forms, Pei was not called on for the exhibition design, carried out by The Burdick Group of San Francisco. The Rock and Roll Hall of Fame is the center-piece of a $300 million development known as North Coast Harbor, which is also to contain a Science Museum and Aquarium designed by other architects.

In the West, the idea of local heritage is quite strong. Antoine Predock certainly took this into account in designing the 12,000 m² American Heritage Center in Laramie, Wyoming. The axis of the project is aligned with two summits – Medicine

I.M. Pei
Rock and Roll Hall of Fame
Cleveland, Ohio, 1993–95
With its pyramidal entrance atrium and projecting geometric volumes, this structure could not be denied by I.M. Pei, yet he may not have been entirely pleased with the interior displays, which he did not design. With its spectacular form and lakeside location, the Rock and Roll Hall of Fame should nonetheless draw in a considerable number of visitors.

Antoine Predock
American Heritage Center
Laramie, Wyoming, 1987–93
Many of Antoine Predock's own
areas of interest, such as UFOs
or the intimate relationship of a
building to its historical and
geological setting, are drawn
together in this unusually shaped
building. Aside from recalling
nearby mountains, the shape may
also remind visitors of Indian
tepees.

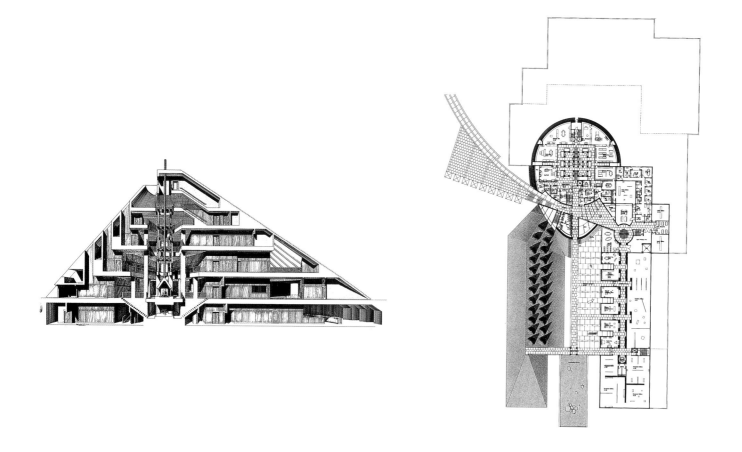

Pages 106/107
Antoine Predock
American Heritage Center
Laramie, Wyoming, 1987–93
Depending on the angle from
which it is viewed, the American
Heritage Center seems to alter-
nate between a highly futuristic
design and an ancient relic.
This type of geologically oriented
modernity is very much on the
mind of other southwestern
American architects such as
Will Bruder.

Bow Peak and Pilot's Knob in the distant Snowy Range and the nearer Laramie Range. As Predock says, this "consciously monumental landscape abstraction represents a symbol for future campus growth . . . and a statement of the powerful spirit of Wyoming." Situated on a 10 ha site, the complex includes the American Heritage Center and Fine Arts Museum. The patinated copper cone at the center of the building corresponds to a nearby round basketball arena, but also calls forth images of a UFO, one of the architect's recurring themes, and is equally reminiscent of a mountainous volcanic shape or a strange warrior's helmet. This example illus-trates Predock's capacity to fuse sources of inspiration that can be at once geolo-gical and anchored in popular culture. The cone and its base house the American Heritage Center, a research facility for scholars. A long, terraced volume with flat roofs, trailing from the cone, houses the University of Wyoming Art Museum, with its collection of artifacts ranging from saddles to mineral maps and stills from Hollywood Westerns. The block-like elements of the museum, intended to recall the architecture of Pueblo Indians, are built with sandblasted concrete blocks specially formed with a coarse aggregate.

The idea of an architecture situated in some sense between the distant past and the imagined future was of course not invented by Antoine Predock. Even the helmet and UFO metaphors are present, for example, in the indoor sports facilities of Fumihiko Maki in Japan. Predock's American Heritage Center is nonetheless a further indication of the liberation of architects to seek new and unusual forms. Such forms are naturally more effective if they carry an element of historical or even geological presence. In fact it seems entirely natural that the cultural sphere would be one in which an effort to bring together the diverse trends and preoccupations of architecture would reach fruition. The projects published here are by no means an exhaustive panorama of new cultural facilities, but they do provide an indication of the breadth and inspiration of current thinking.

PLACES OF GATHERING

Congress, Worship, Sport and Study

Page 109
Massimiliano Fuksas
Montaigne University
Art School Building
Bordeaux, France, 1993–94
Calling on a patinated copper finish with very few visible openings, which emphasizes the sculptural quality of this building, Fuksas highlights his own belief in the increasingly close connection between art and architecture. Stating his admiration for artists like the Italian painter Fontana, he composed this building with a minimalist vocabulary.

Page 110
Massimiliano Fuksas
Montaigne University
Art School Building
Bordeaux, France, 1993–94
A collage and watercolor work by the architect provides a final idea of the structure in an unusual mode of expression. Once again, he thus emphasizes a relationship between the built form and its two-dimensional, artistic representation, an approach that seems to run against the prevailing tendency to call more and more on computers.

Museums as such have certainly offered ample opportunities to modern architects to express themselves quite freely. Over recent years, however there has been a trend to group cultural functions together in complex centers such as Arata Isozaki's Art Tower Mito in Japan or, in a different vein, Richard Meier's ambitious Getty Center. Both of these centers include spaces for the exhibition of art, but their program goes far beyond that of a museum. Indeed places of gathering, whether cultural or intended for congress and worship, whether meant for sporting events or as schools and libraries, represent a wide field whose inherently demonstrative nature encourages authorities to call more than in the past on well-known architects. As in other types of construction, these facilities have been subjected to rigorous budgetary constraints, and have benefited from the ability of architects to design innovative forms, specifically adapted to circumstances, and often produced through the intermediary of computer-aided design.

Congress and Worship

Two buildings by the Japanese architect Tadao Ando, one situated in Europe and the other in Japan, illustrate the variety of small places of gathering conceived by contemporary architects in recent years. The first, the Vitra Conference Pavilion (Weil am Rhein, Germany, 1992–93), is situated in the midst of the Vitra furniture factory complex, where Frank O. Gehry, Zaha Hadid, Nicholas Grimshaw and Alvaro Siza have also worked. This small structure, with a ground floor of 420 m^2, a first floor of 218 m^2 and a basement measuring 202 m^2, is made of concrete, American oak and glass. Concrete is of course Ando's favorite construction material, and this structure proves his ability to obtain excellent quality, even outside of his native Japan. Ando's own words about the building give some sense of his approach: "The building stands on land of almost unvarying flatness, with a cover of cherry trees. When first visiting the site, I was struck by the quality of 'movement' that the Frank O. Gehry Design Museum projected so powerfully. Opposite Gehry's architecture of 'movement,' I introduced the element of 'stillness.' Choosing the most static of all forms – the square – I employed it in the plan of a sunken court, inset into the flat site . . . By thus engaging the buildings in a relationship of tension, my ultimate aim was to produce a place of strongly provocative character." Indeed, the alignment of Ando's structure *vis-à-vis* the Gehry museum is such that it is impossible to see the museum from within the conference pavilion. It would seem that the tension sought by Ando is a case of rejection here as well.

Ando's Buddhist Hompuku-ji Temple, on the island of Awaji in Japan, does not suffer from the same kind of architectural rivalry. Although integrated into an existing monastery, it sits with an unobstructed view of the Bay of Osaka. Unexpectedly, the hall of the temple itself is placed beneath an oval-shaped lotus basin, reached through a descending staircase that bisects the basin. Before reaching this entry, the visitor is obliged to go around a long and quite remarkable concrete wall. Clearly, here, as in Weil am Rhein and in other structures that he has

built, Ando seeks to make the visitor aware that he is entering a sacred space. Once in the temple, the visitor encounters a red pillared hall with a Buddha placed in the center, its back to the west, where a single corner opening allows the entry of natural light. At the end of the day, light floods the hall. Although not large, this structure certainly gives an impression of religious space. It is a place of meeting, but above all, a place of worship. Ando's strength is to show that the use of a strictly Modernist geometric vocabulary, with materials often considered to be very ordinary, such as concrete, does permit a remarkable spirituality to be expressed. Ando has done as much for Christian chapels, so it might be said that the spiritual element uncovered here is more probably an enlightened sense of late twentieth century humanism. Ando, despite frequent criticism, is undeniably one of the great architects of the late twentieth century, with an importance that already has been projected beyond his homeland.

Another Japanese architect of indisputable refinement and talent is 1993 Pritzker Prize winner Fumihiko Maki. Two of his buildings, the Tokyo Metropolitan Gymnasium, and Tepia, also located in the Japanese capital, show how skillfully this architect has been able to blend the lessons of Modernism, the architectural tradition of his country, and the demands of contemporary buildings. The gymnasium is a centrally located 44,000 m^2 complex with a main arena, indoor swimming pool and smaller arena. The roof of the main structure, a 120 m long oval, recalls Maki's 1984 Fujisawa Gymnasium, which also brought to mind the image of a samurai's helmet or a flying saucer. Maki also compares the shape to an oyster's shell. Tepia, located nearby, is a 14,000 m^2 structure erected for meetings organized by the Japanese ministry of industry (MITI), whose exterior cladding is a 5 mm thick gray aluminum. Here the sweeping curves seen in the gymnasium are replaced by a rectilinear geometry apparently influenced by the Dutch de Stijl movement. Despite this European reference, the subtle alternation between opacity, translucence and transparency

Pages 112/113
Tadao Ando
Vitra Seminar and Study Center
Weil am Rhein, Germany, 1992–93
With his first permanent built work in Europe, Ando did not abandon his predilection for concrete, nor his taste for an unusual entry path, which recalls Japanese temples and makes the visitor notice the building he is about to enter. Although it is located next to Gehry's Vitra Design Museum, Ando's building notably turns a blind eye in that direction, preferring to focus on the views of the surrounding natural setting.

seen in this building marks a clear relation to the Japanese tradition of the screen, although these effects are attained with very modern materials such as perforated aluminum. As Maki says, it would be impossible for any architect to impose a sense of order on the apparently chaotic urban environment that is Tokyo, but the quiet elegance and understated strength of Tepia shows that Japanese architecture is fully capable of attaining the delicate equilibrium between past and future that is surely the most significant hallmark of the best in contemporary buildings.

Three recent buildings and one computer-generated project give an idea of the evolution of the architecture of places of congress and worship in Europe.

Richard Meier's Stadthaus civic center in Ulm, Germany, was dedicated on November 12, 1993. The 3,500 m² three-story complex clad in Rosa Dante granite and white stucco, without any metal panels, houses exhibition spaces, a large assembly hall, a café and a tourist information center. It is notable not only for its own design, but also for the ways in which Richard Meier has resolved the complex problems posed by the site in the Münsterplatz, which he was also called upon to redesign. The historic center of this town of 100,000 is dominated by the 161 m tall Ulm Münster Cathedral. Eighty-five percent of the historic city was destroyed by

Tadao Ando
Hompuku-ji Temple
Awajishima, Japan, 1989–90
The entrance to this temple leads
the visitor to the curving concrete
wall seen to the left, before he
discovers the artificial pond and
the stairs, which lead down into
the temple itself. There, a representation of Buddha sits, with its
back to the setting sun.

Fumihiko Maki
Tokyo Metropolitan Gymnasium
Tokyo, Japan, 1986–90
Variously described as resembling
a samurai's helmet, a scarab
beetle or a UFO, this 43,971 m²
facility is situated on a 4 ha site in
the Meiji Park. Its main arena has
a seating capacity of 10,000, and
there is an indoor swimming pool
with spectator seating for 900.
Continually changing views out
to the neighboring park and city
open up as one moves between
the dynamically juxtaposed
building masses.

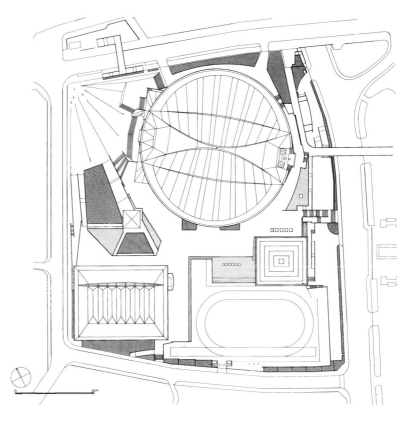

bombing in 1944, and the reconstruction of Ulm was carried out without much regard for the quality of the architecture. The curving, pedestrian Bahnhofstrasse leads from the train station to the square, where Meier has placed a curved wall that leads people into the square. A glass bridge with a pedestrian underpass links the two basic elements of the structure, facilitating the penetration of the space, as do the numerous possible points of entry into the building itself. As Meier points out, one of the interesting features of the building is the proliferation of points of view throughout the building toward the cathedral spire. Undeniably successful, Meier's Ulm Stadthaus shows that modern forms need not be contradictory with historic environments, even in the densely packed context of old European cities. This note of clarity and order in fact greatly improves the city center of Ulm, which was not rebuilt with much concern for architectural quality after the war. This is a place of congress which in many ways gives Ulm its own heart back. It is an urban center of gravity, predicated on the neighboring cathedral, but resolutely of our time.

Mario Botta's Cathedral in Evry (1992–95) faces a related problem in giving a center to a new city, created without any real sense of urban design. Located just to the south of Paris, Evry is a rather ugly modern town. Calling on the truncated cylindrical form that he seems to favor, Botta erected this 4,800 m^2 church with a reinforced concrete structure and brick cladding on both the exterior and interior. The apparently unusual form of the cathedral, a 38.5 m circular plan, in fact makes reference to Byzantine churches, and in this respect looks back to the origins of Christianity. An unusual triangular metal frame carries the roof structure, admitting generous amounts of daylight, making the interior very agreeable if not as obviously spiritual as in Ando's chapels for example. Criticized as a costly venture that the church could ill afford, this cathedral, the first built in France for more than a century, in fact proclaims the living faith shared by parishioners in this modern context. With the square in front of it, the Evry cathedral gives some sense of a center to this *ville nouvelle,* which is otherwise devoid of architectural common sense.

Rem Koolhaas and the Office for Metropolitan Architecture (OMA) were chosen to design the master plan of the Euralille complex in Lille, France, in November 1988. Physically separated from the rest of the buildings designed by Jean Nouvel Christian de Portzamparc, Claude Vasconi and Jean-Marie Duthilleul, the Grand Palais conference center and exhibition hall by Koolhaas is surrounded by heavily traveled roads. With a total of 50,000 m^2 of usable space and a 350 million franc budget, the Grand Palais certainly deserves its name. The 300 m long oval structure includes a 15,000 seat rock concert hall (Zénith), three auditoriums, an 18,000 m^2 wide open exhibition hall, and parking for 1,200 cars. The first of impression of the visitor who enters the building is one of surprise. A great deal of exposed concrete and a large corrugated plastic "column of light" lead to an astonishing double staircase. Plastic, plywood and other inexpensive materials are indeed the hallmark of the Grand Palais, for budgetary reasons, but it is a measure of the talent of Koolhaas that he has turned this problem into an interesting design feature of the structure. As for the master plan of Euralille, Koolhaas has explained that the internal complexity of the Grand Palais means that it has urban design *on the inside.* The theories of "urban congestion" elaborated by Rem Koolhaas conclude that it is useless to try to impose any order on urban sprawl, and that it is much more constructive to live with the inherent disorder of the city. This unusual stance may well find fruitful application in truly large cities such as New York, Tokyo or Jakarta, but Lille has no such dimension. That said, the concentration of facilities, from office towers to a shopping center and the Grand Palais itself near the Eurostar rail station in Lille, make for a place of meeting that undoubtedly will enrich the life of this northern city. The successful use of inexpensive materials in a large-scale structure also shows what a talented architect is capable of doing with rather drastic economic constraints.

Pages 116/117
Fumihiko Maki
Tepia
Tokyo, Japan, 1985–89
Occupied by MITI (Ministry of International Trade and Industry), this pavilion for science and high technology is located next to the Meiji Park in the Minato-ku area of Tokyo. As Maki says, "The high standard of technology and craftsmanship maintained by Japan's system of building and construction has made this design and its details possible. In all likelihood, an equivalent level of technology and craftsmanship may not endure indefinitely; thus Tepia is in a sense a testimony to Japanese society of today."

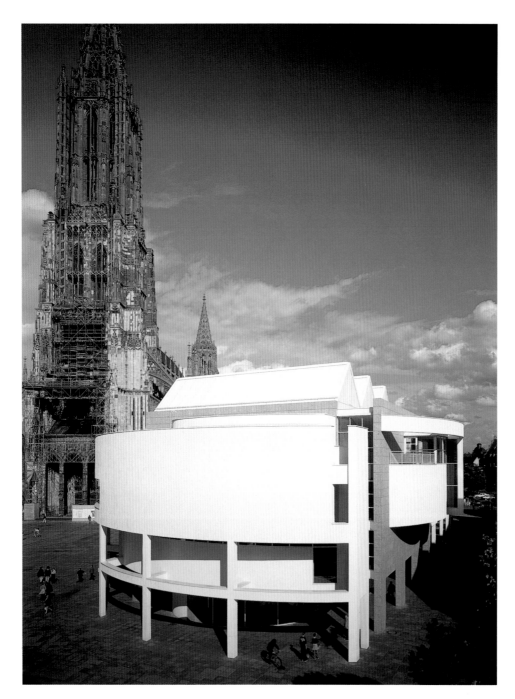

Christian de Portzamparc, author of one of the towers in the Euralille complex, is also in the process of rebuilding the Paris Palais des Congrès, located at the Porte Maillot in the French capital. The program includes the refurbishment of 13,606 m^2 of existing spaces, and the creation of 49,915 m^2 including exhibition spaces, offices and a 550-seat conference room for the Paris Chamber of Commerce. This extra space is to be obtained by moving the facade forward and restructuring the very busy Porte Maillot roundabout. The facade itself will be skewed forward, with large openings and external signs offering a clear hint of what is going on within. Because of its sensitivity to the urban environment in this admittedly difficult site, where there is little neighboring architecture, the Palais de Congrès project, visualized through the form of computer-generated perspectives, represents an interesting solution to the frequently posed problem of adaptive reuse in city centers.

Pages 118/119
Richard Meier
Exhibition and Assembly Building
Ulm, Germany, 1986–93
This 3,500 m² complex is located next to the Ulm Münster Cathedral with its celebrated 161 m spire, which was spared in the saturation bombing of 1944 that destroyed eighty-five percent of the city. Meier, who was also called on to redesign the square itself, has succeeded well in integrating his modern, geometric design into this irregular and historically important setting.

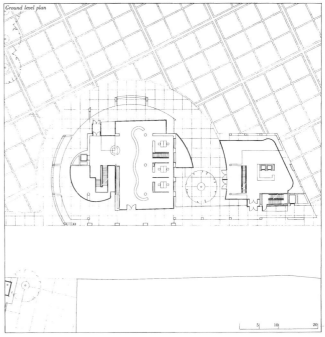

Ground level plan

Pages 120/121
Mario Botta
Évry Cathedral
Évry, France, 1988–95

Located just south of Paris, Évry is a *ville nouvelle* or new city, which was built with very little sense of urban planning. The new cathedral and the square in front of it give at least a point of convergence to the local residents. Here, as in San Francisco, the architect has used a truncated cone as the main design element of this Byzantine-plan church, with individually laid bricks in the simple, powerful interior.

Christian de Portzamparc
Palais des Congrès, Porte Maillot
Paris, France, 1996–2000
This design for an extension and refurbishment of the Porte Maillot convention center is located on an extremely busy roundabout on the axis leading from the Champs-Élysées to the Défense area of Paris. Using computer-aided design, the architect has added a volume that is raked forward, toward the roundabout, with large-scale signs announcing current events.

Dominique Perrault
**Bibliothèque nationale de France
Paris, France, 1988–96**
With its four towers in the shape of open volumes situated around a large sunken garden, the Bibliothèque nationale de France was subject to a great deal of controversy, some of which was politically motivated, and some of which had to do with the probability that high glass towers were not the best form for the conservation of precious books. Modified to respond to criticism, the project has recently been more favorably viewed in France.

Libraries and Schools

As culturally oriented buildings, libraries and schools have also been high on the list of the types of buildings that talented contemporary architects are asked to design. After the art museum, the library may be one of the most potent symbols of cultural achievement and intellectual prowess. Although London has long been working on the new British Library, the most spectacular and largest library project anywhere in the world is most probably the last of the *Grands Travaux* of François Mitterrand. The so-called Bibliothèque nationale de France is located in the 13th arrondissement of Paris in a zone formerly occupied essentially by the rail lines leading to the Austerlitz train station. With its 450 km of bookshelves and 4,000 seats in the lecture rooms this 360,000 m² building stands out if only because of its size. The concept of four 100 m high towers placed like "open books" around a central sunken garden was vigorously attacked by a number of eminent specialists, not only because of the obvious difficulty in retrieving books placed in towers, but also because of the danger to the volumes exposed to light and heat in structures that were originally intended to be highly transparent. The project was modified to

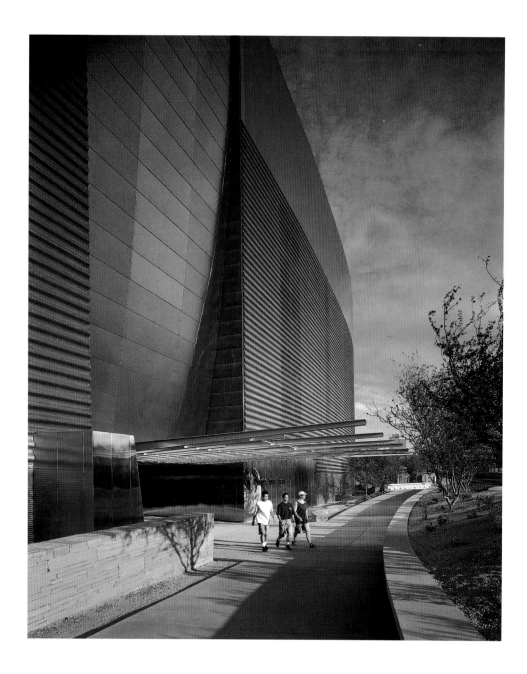

Pages 124/125
Will Bruder
Phoenix Central Library
Phoenix, Arizona, 1988–95
With a relatively low $97.60 per
square foot cost, this library deserves more than a little attention
in Europe, where massive and
costly libraries have been erected,
most notably in London and Paris.
Related to its surroundings
through the architect's sense of
local geology, the building's profile is extremely modern, and it is
undoubtedly well suited internally
to the evolution toward new
media that public libraries are
now encountering.

reduce the height of the towers, to better protect the volumes kept in them, and to increase the size of the stacks situated in the base of the complex. Despite a Modernist concept based in good part on the architect's admiration for Minimalist artists like Carl André and Richard Serra, the harsh aspects of the Bibliothèque are somewhat softened by the central garden, visible essentially from the reading rooms. By creating this sunken font of greenery, Dominique Perrault intended to make reference to the Garden of Eden, to the Original Sin and thus to the origin of the knowledge contained in the millions of volumes kept here. Many critics have retained only the Modernist geometry of the towers to criticize this project as being behind the times in terms of architectural thinking, but the strong presence of the library, especially as viewed from within, indeed its very size, makes it a project to be reckoned with. There is certainly a case to be made for the fact that a simple analysis of its geometry is not sufficient to grasp the nature of this building. The central garden is an unusual aspect, as is the frequent use of unusual materials, such as a kind of "chain mail" stainless steel ceiling material within. Perrault himself points out that Modernist buildings rarely made a point of digging into the earth, as does his sunken garden. Rather, like Le Corbusier's Villa Savoye, they tended to want to rise about the ground, either on pilotis or by sitting lightly on their sites. In an almost Freudian way, Perrault claims that the Bibliothèque is far removed from

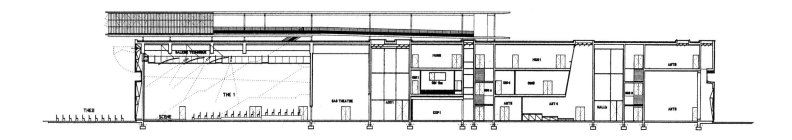

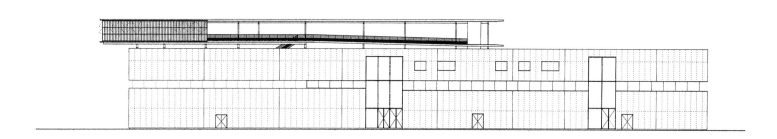

the modern purist tenants, and he may be right about that. In any case, through massive intervention of the French government, a new place of intellectual gathering has been created in Paris.

Another urban symbol of significance is the new Phoenix Public Library designed by Will Bruder. This structure is intended to serve as the central library of Phoenix, Arizona, until at least 2040, and presently contains over one million volumes. No less than 40,000 kg of ribbed copper cladding cover the exterior of this 26,000 m² library, especially on the east and west facades. The southern elevation is entirely glass covered. Inside, the ground floor combines current fiction, audio, video, computing, a children's reading room, a theater, and a café. The library's services are spread on five floors with copper-clad mechanical and service "saddlebags," which protect the interior from the extremely hot desert sun. The most spectacular interior space is the fifth-floor 4,000 m² reading room, housing the entire collection of circulating non-fiction books. Arrival to this "great room" is via glass elevators or a grand sculptural staircase of steel, concrete and translucent glass. At the center of the building, there is a five-story atrium/light well, which Bruder has dubbed the "Crystal Canyon". As this name makes clear, the architect intends this building to have a close relationship to geology. Born in 1946, Will Bruder was self-trained as an architect, but his early apprenticeship under Paolo Soleri and Gunnar Birkerts gives some hint of what he calls his "pursuit of 'architecture as art' married to a hands-on sense of reality." As in the case of Predock's Laramie building, copper is an important element in the cladding of the new Phoenix structure, but here the scale is larger. Bruder's own description of the building makes clear his intentions: "Arizona's natural beauty provides the poetic metaphor for the library's image. A majestic mesa transplanted from the fantastic landscape of Arizona's Monument Valley... The building's exterior appearance is original rather than traditional, rather like a geological landform or abstract minimalist sculpture." Both Bruder's reference to "architecture as art" and this last comparison to "abstract minimalist sculpture" relate his work to the trends already demonstrated for architects as different as Frank O. Gehry and Steven Holl. Coming from the Southwest, where urban growth has been strong and the remarkable landscape is never far removed, Bruder, like Predock, calls on a more distant past than any architectural tradition. This search goes back even farther than the "primitivist" exploration of the early mod-

Pages 126/127
Massimiliano Fuksas
Montaigne University
Art School Building
Bordeaux, France, 1993–94
Contrasting with the patinated copper used for most of the cladding, Massimiliano Fuksas decided to use strips of wood to cover the perched volume of the campus radio station, which is cantilevered forward, above the mass of the sculptural base. Lit from the interior, it becomes even lighter in appearance at night.

ern artists to touch fundamental elements that are still very much part of everyday life in this area of the United States.

Naturally, not all libraries take on the huge dimensions and mythological ambitions of the Bibliothèque nationale de France or the Phoenix Public Library. Much more modest structures do exist, as is the case for example of the Towell Temporary Library on the UCLA Brentwood campus by Hodgetts + Fung, already mentioned above. Here a lightweight architecture, which is naturally easier to conceive in a benevolent climate such as that of Los Angeles, houses a light-filled and highly functional library space.

Although not in such an obvious way as museums or libraries, schools have also provided occasions for architecture to further its development in recent years. The new Arts Center of the Michel de Montaigne University in Bordeaux, France (1993–94), is a case in point. Designed by the Italian architect Massimiliano Fuksas, it is intended to bring together different disciplines, such as theater, music sculpture, radio and cinema. A long, narrow building, cut in half lengthwise and pierced by two large vertical shafts, it is clad in a skin of light green oxidized copper. The radio studio is positioned on the roof and is clad in wood. Fuksas feels that contemporary architecture is more and more influenced by art. He cites the Italian painter Lucio Fontana as a personal favorite, but it is clear that the sculptural presence of his Bordeaux art school owes much to sculpture as well. The gathering of different artistic disciplines in this structure obviously pleads in favor of his own belief that architecture itself is now in a position to reclaim its true identity as an art form. A skilled practitioner with extensive experience in the construction of low-cost housing, Fuksas is far from a dilettante, and his concept and the explanation he gives for it here should be considered as significant of wider trends in architecture.

Three teaching facilities built in Tokyo in the past ten years exploit different approaches to the problems of the relationship between education and architecture. The most remarkable and important of these is undoubtedly Kazuo Shinohara's Tokyo Institute of Technology, Centennial Hall, located in the Meguro area of the Japanese capital. Completed in 1987, it indeed corresponds to the architect's description which was of a "machine floating in the air." Calling on the Japanese architectural tradition of undefined spaces, Shinohara created a 20 m high space to be used for exhibitions or other university functions. With bare concrete walls and exposed piping, electrical lines and air conditioning ducts, this area has an industrial aspect, which is due in good part to the low construction budget. Above, the building is bisected by its most obvious feature, a slanted semi-cylindrical volume, which houses a restaurant. Apparently disordered, the Centennial Hall corresponds at once to Shinohara's thoughts about the underlying order of the Japanese metropolis and to his examination of machines like the Lunar Landing Module (LEM) or the American F-14 fighter plane. The "terrifying efficiency" of these machines means, as far as Shinohara is concerned, that it is not necessarily a straightforward geometric composition that best corresponds to the function and appearance of a building. Making reference to recent scientific "chaos theory," the seventy year old Shinohara, who has had considerable influence on younger Japanese architects like Toyo Ito and Itsuko Hasegawa, predicts that the forms of the future of architecture will have more to do with new perceptions of efficiency than they will with outdated concepts of esthetic harmony.

Esthetic harmony is certainly far from the mind of Makoto Watanabe, a forty-five year old architect, whose 1990 Aoyama Technical College building in Tokyo looks like something out of Japanese cartoons. Seeking an "organic" architecture in other crystalline designs, Watanabe here seems fascinated by the mechanical or robotic metaphor. His school looks like it could get up and walk away, fitting easily into a "Godzilla" movie or "Power Rangers" television feature. He certainly does not reject the notion that popular culture is a source of inspiration for this highly

Kazuo Shinohara
Centennial Hall,
Tokyo Institute of Technology
Tokyo, Japan, 1985–87
This striking building stands out against a typically Japanese urban environment, which is visually chaotic. Its internal wiring and plumbing is all left visible for reasons of cost, but such details confirm the place of this structure as a prototypical design for the "Post-Bubble" period of the Japanese economy, which intervened only in the 1990s and ended the trend toward excessively costly buildings.

Makoto Sei Watanabe
Aoyama Art School
Tokyo, Japan, 1988–90
Like a mechanical creature that
just strode out of a Goldorak
cartoon, this art school saves
most of its visual effects for the
exterior. Its interior is generally
relatively unremarkable. This
type of design is typical of the
speculative euphoria of the late
1980s in Japan.

unusual building. Despite an apparent rejection of the formalist vocabulary used by
slightly older architects like Ando, Watanabe does not seem that far in his concep-
tions from the radical chaos-oriented theories of Shinohara.

Kijo Rokkaku's 17,604 m² Tokyo Budokan, completed in December 1989, is a
school of a different kind. Here it is judo, archery or other traditional Japanese
sports that are taught. Rejecting traditional materials and direct reference to
architectural history, Rokkaku sought his inspiration for the facade of this building
in the forms of mountain ranges. His careful choice of materials and the juxtaposition of the different elements nonetheless give a very Japanese feeling to this
building, which is naturally heightened by the presence of persons of all ages
practicing traditional sports.

Kijo Rokkaku
Tokyo Budokan
Tokyo, Japan, 1987–89

Despite its complex, modern appearance, this facility is intended essentially for traditional sports such as archery or judo. The crystalline design of the facade is carried through in such internal devices as triangular space frames like that visible in the archery range above.

Cultural Centers and Concert Halls

The trend toward cultural centers intended for a wide variety of uses has certainly been strong in Japan, and the challenge of giving a coherent shape to such multi-use complexes has been met with ingenuity by the Japanese and foreign architects called on to build them. One striking example is the Shonandai Cultural Center, located in Fujisawa near Tokyo. The work of Itsuko Hasegawa, one of the most successful female architects in the country, the Shonandai Center explicitly rejects the reductive formalism of architects like Ando. This is an "inclusive" architecture, which seeks nothing else than to mimic the universe. Globes representing the heavens and the earth are the dominating shapes, with a symbolic river emerging from the South Pole of the earth, and running through the middle of a complex square, which includes aluminum trees. Ninety percent of the 11,028 m² of the center are located below grade in a surprisingly functional Modernist "box" type of arrangement. From the brightly colored marbles included in the aluminum chairs she designed for Shonandai to the "landscape" of the outlying walls derived from her vision of the typical Japanese countryside, this is an inventive and playful world onto itself. Although this type of complexity may not be the most fashionable expression of contemporary architecture, it is an indication of the emerging talent of women architects, and quite a joyful place for children to learn about science, or for older women to learn the art of *ikebana* or pottery making.

Arata Isozaki's Art Tower Mito, located in Mito, again near Tokyo, is clearly visible from a large distance because of its spiraling 100 m tower. More than anything a symbolic gesture meant to call attention to the complex, the tower was most

Pages 132/133
Itsuko Hasegawa
Shonandai Cultural Center
Fujisawa, Kanagawa, Japan,
1987–91
Intended as a reduced-scale model of the universe, this complex, which includes a museum for children, classrooms and auditoriums, is certainly the most widely published of Hasegawa's works. Her vocabulary of perforated aluminum and concrete landscaping is meant to evoke the idea of an artificial replica of nature, undoubtedly a useful concept in the urban chaos of Japan.

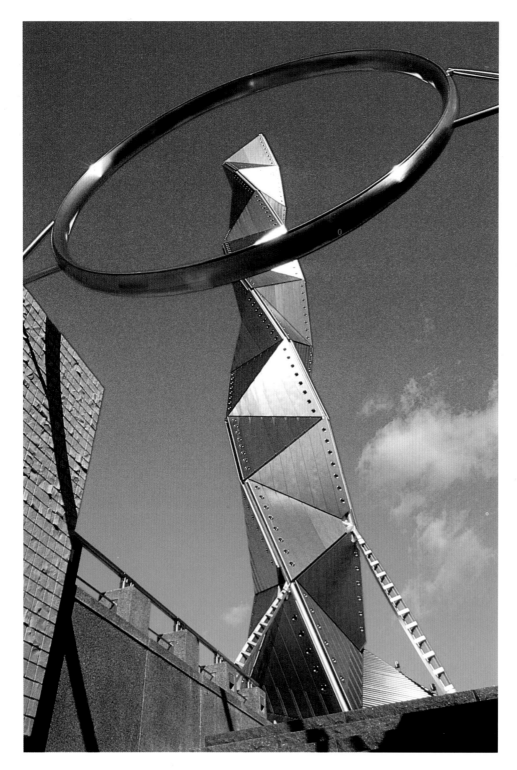

probably to some extent inspired by the similarly designed paper lamps conceived by Isozaki's friend, the late sculptor Isamu Noguchi. It also bears a certain resemblance to Brancusi's "Colonne sans fin." Though its form is certainly distant from that of the Centre Pompidou in Paris, it seems clear that the intellectual model for the mixed-use cultural center, here including an exhibition space, concert halls and a No theater stage, is indeed French. The Art Tower Mito is redolent with historic references, from Sir John Soane to Claude Nicolas Ledoux, but as the architect says in typically humorous fashion, "Every element is treated in a schizophrenic manner, so the whole becomes coherent." Isozaki certainly went through a Post-Modern period, most notably with his 1983 Tsukuba Center, but here, despite the numerous indirect historic references, he has already gone beyond the Post-Modern pastiche to create an unusual work of art. The culminating point of Art Tower Mito is pre-

Rafael Viñoly
Tokyo International Forum
Tokyo, Japan, 1989–96
Located close to the Tokyo
JR Railway Station, this enormous
130,000 m² complex will have cost
more than $1.6 billion to build.
Chosen from amongst 395 entries
from fifty different countries,
the project of Rafael Viñoly
features the largest theater in
Tokyo (5,000 seats) as well as a
Glass Hall measuring 191 m in
length, 30 m in width and no
less than 57 m in height.

cisely its tower, and as Isozaki points out, despite some investigation in this direction by Buckminster Fuller, there is no architectural equivalent of the form of this tower. Surrounded by European references, it rises above them and creates a new, sculptural presence on the low skyline of this otherwise architecturally undistinguished suburb.

Another, even more ambitious cultural center is being completed in the Marunouchi District of Tokyo, facing the outer Gardens of the Imperial Palace to the west. Rafael Viñoly's Tokyo International Forum is situated on a 3 ha site where the Tokyo City Hall and City Council Building was formerly located, and will accommodate dance, musical and theatrical performances, conventions and trade shows, business meetings and receptions. It will also house offices, cultural information centers and public spaces. Viñoly was selected by a jury that included I.M. Pei,

Fumihiko Maki, Kenzo Tange, Vittorio Gregotti and Arthur Erickson in November 1989, which is to say before the speculative real estate "bubble" broke in Japan. This explains the extremely ambitious nature of this project, whose form consists of two intersecting glass and steel ellipses enclosing an enormous central lobby. With a total floor area of over 130,000 m², and a project cost exceeding $1 billion, the Tokyo International Forum may indeed be the most expensive and vast building of its type in the world. The elliptical shapes of the structure confer a fundamental geometric simplicity to this building, which places it very much in the current stream of architectural thought, despite the relatively long period between its initial conception and the 1996 completion.

One consequence of the numerous competitions held in Japan and elsewhere to design cultural facilities is that a large number of talented architects have thought about this problem. Even their unchosen, unbuilt works are interesting in this respect, and may often have an influence despite not being completed. Such is the case with the French architect Christian de Portzamparc's Nara Convention Center project. In this 1992 competition, won by Arata Isozaki, architects were asked to design a group of three halls: a 2,000-seat convention and show space, a 500-seat concert hall and a 100-seat multi-use hall. This was one of Portzamparc's first ventures into computer-aided design, and his elegant project shows the influence of this mode of thinking on the forms of the project.

Fumihiko Maki's Kirishima Concert Hall, mentioned above, is just one stunning example to prove that not every new cultural building in Japan is conceived in the multi-use pattern of Art Tower Mito. Here the musical function is clearly announced and preserved, and Maki has shown that elegance, Japanese tradition and a fundamentally traditional program can be blended into a stunning contemporary building.

On the other side of the Pacific, in San Francisco, Maki is also responsible for the very successful Yerba Buena Center, located just across Third Street from Mario Botta's San Francisco Museum of Modern Art. Necessarily light in its conception because it is built over underground spaces of the nearby Moscone Convention Center, the Yerba Buena building is like an aluminum ship, docked near the Yerba Buena park. Unfortunately, despite the proximity of Botta and Maki in this instance, with a theater built by James Stewart Polshek also very close by, there seems to have been very little cooperation and contact between the architects. Although this might be deemed to be the responsibility of the public authorities involved in the planning of the projects, it is significant of contemporary architecture that true cooperation, especially between such well-known figures, is rather rare. For those who keep score in such instances, it would seem obvious that Maki's light and flexible Yerba Buena Center is architecturally more successful than Botta's heavy and rather mausoleum-like brick veneer museum.

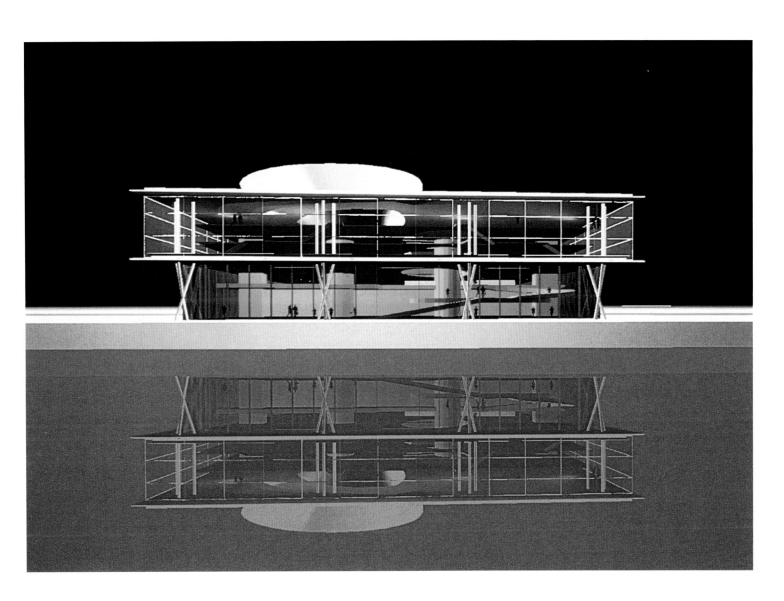

Above
Christian de Portzamparc
Cultural Center
Copenhagen, Denmark,
1993 (project)

Right
Christian de Portzamparc
Nara Convention Hall
Nara, Japan, 1992 (project)
The red computer drawing represents a proposal for a flower-
shaped concert hall with 600 seats
whose form is in fact derived from
that of a Möbius strip. Although
neither one of these entries was
finally selected, such projects do
tend to affirm the international
presence of an architect and
make it more likely that he will
be selected in the future.

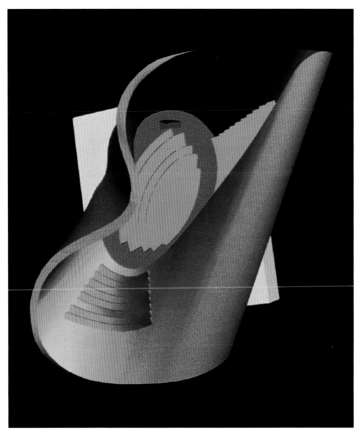

Again, with the constraints imposed by recession and other financial difficulties, California is one of the most active areas in the United States for new cultural facilities. The most impressive of these by far is Richard Meier's Getty Center, located on a spectacular wind-swept site midway between the Pacific and downtown Los Angeles. The very figures give an impression of the size of this project. Its estimated cost is $733 million, with the site preparation alone costing $115 million. The new Getty Center will provide 87,800 m^2 of space excluding entrance and parking facilities. The complex will cover 9.7 ha of the 44.5 ha site. An adjoining 243 ha owned by the Getty Trust will preserve the natural quality of the area. In many respects, this is the largest project granted to a single architect in the late twentieth century. And the first impressions of it confirms that it will mark the period in more ways than one. "In my mind's eye," Richard Meier has said, "I see a classic structure, elegant and timeless, emerging, serene and ideal, from the rough hillside, a kind of Aristotelian structure within the landscape. Sometimes I think that the landscape overtakes it, and sometimes I see the structure as standing out, dominating the landscape; the two are entwined in a dialogue, a perpetual embrace in which building and site are one. In my mind I keep returning to the Romans – to Hadrian's Villa, to Caprarola – for their sequence of spaces, their thick-walled presence, their sense of order, the way in which building and landscape belong to each other."

Fumihiko Maki
Yerba Buena Center for the Arts
San Francisco, California, 1991–93
Visible in the foreground of the image to the left above (Botta's SFMoMA structure is in the rear), this is Maki's first building designed in the United States in more than 30 years. Because of the limitations the underground Moscone Center imposed on the site, the Center for the Arts is forced literally to float within its dense urban context.

Frank O. Gehry
Disney Concert Hall
Los Angeles, California,
1988– (project)
Located just down the street
from Arata Isozaki's Museum of
Contemporary Art, the Disney
Concert Hall, hailed as Frank O.
Gehry's first really large building
in the United States has unfortunately not yet been built due to
cost-related factors. It remains
an intriguing and undoubtedly
influential design.

Set above the San Diego Freeway, the Getty already stands out like a fortress or a monastery above Los Angeles. This is in part due to the vast retaining walls clad in cleft travertine. This Italian stone strikes an entirely new note in the architecture of Richard Meier, and highlights the deep connections that his architecture has always had to the monuments of the past. Various forms of local opposition obliged the architect to abandon his trademark white surfaces. Even the metal panels used here will have a light beige tone. Although he insists on the "Italian hill town" aspect of the design, the complex as it is being built does have a rather remote appearance, which is clearly alleviated as the visitor reaches the esplanade in front of the Museum. With its facilities not only for the J. Paul Getty Museum but also for the numerous other activities of the Getty Trust, this mountaintop monastery of a cultural center will be only partially open to the public. It will also conserve a function of research and scientific study. As such it is unique, and perhaps unlikely to serve as a model for any other institution in the foreseeable future. In architectural terms, many critics have said that it will be a 1980s building completed at the turn of the century, and as such out of phase with newer trends. Known as a dyed-in-the-wool Modernist with a strict geometric vocabulary usually expressed only in his trade-mark white, Meier does nonetheless succeed here in operating a delicate transition toward a period in which deep-seated references to historic tradition or even geological presence are expressed.

A more complex case is that of Frank O. Gehry's Disney Concert Hall. Situated near Arata Isozaki's Museum of Contemporary Art, this home for the L.A. Phil-harmonic should be clad in limestone, like the American Center in Paris. Its form has been compared to an "exploding rose," and this complex shape led to a certain amount of criticism. Due to projected cost overruns and the inability of fund raisers to find a complement to the $50 million given in 1987 by Walt Disney's widow Lillian B. Disney, it has been suggested that the building might be clad in gray titanium as opposed to the more expensive limestone. As of the end of 1995, with a budgetary shortfall estimated at between $80 million and $120 million (according to *Newsweek*), the construction of the concert hall had not advanced beyond the underground parking lot.

In Europe, although many other examples of multi-use cultural facilities exist, one of the most interesting is Jean Nouvel's Fondation Cartier, located in Paris. Art exhibitions, small concerts, theater and other cultural events can all be held in this

Pages 140/141
Jean Nouvel
Fondation Cartier
Paris, France, 1991–94
Located on the site of the former American Center on the Boulevard Raspail, Nouvel's Fondation Cartier confirms his reputation as one of the two leading contemporary French architects. The transparency and multiple layering of the structure take Modernist tenets one step further, although the enormous glass volume on the ground floor may not be ideally suited to the display of works of art.

large open space. "I place art in architecture, and architecture in the city," says Jean Nouvel, chosen by the GAN insurance company (owner of the land) and Cartier to build the new Fondation Cartier building at 261 Boulevard Raspail in Paris in 1991. The structure includes no fewer than sixteen levels, of which eight are below grade. There are 4,000 m² of offices for Cartier France, 1,600 m² of exhibition space for the Foundation, 800 m² of technical space, and 4,000 m² of gardens. Most importantly, the Fondation Cartier is made up of some 5,000 m² of glass facades. As Nouvel, says, "It is an architecture whose game is to make the tangible limits of the structure disappear in a poetically evanescent manner. When the virtual and the real are no longer distinct, architecture must have the courage to assume such a contradiction." Nouvel, whose own striking black silhouette seems carefully calculated to contribute to his image as a living legend, certainly thinks highly of his own work, but his excellent opinion of himself does seem to be borne out by the Fondation Cartier, one of the most innovative and striking buildings erected in France in recent years.

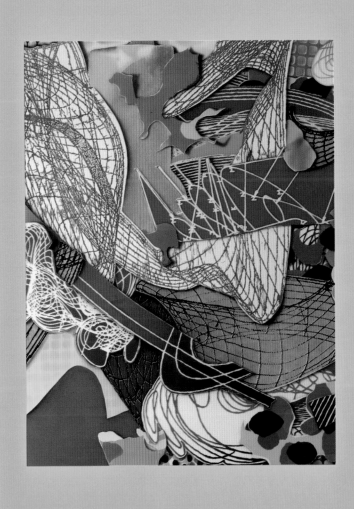

Breaking down the Barriers

As has already been suggested above in several specific cases, one change that has occurred in recent years is that art and architecture have drawn closer together. In a sense, this movement seems only natural. As John Ruskin said, "No person who is not a great sculptor or painter can be an architect. If he is not a sculptor or painter, he can only be a builder." The twentieth century has been rich in movements combining painting, sculpture and architecture, from De Stijl and the Bauhaus to ambitious if misguided efforts to use all of the arts to the ends of propaganda in Germany, the Soviet Union or Italy from the late 1920s to the war years. Major international exhibitions such as the one held in Paris in 1937 were showcases for this kind of synthesis of the arts, with Albert Speer's monumental German pavilion or the more interesting Spanish pavilion, designed by Josep Lluis Sert, containing work by the sculptors Julio Gonzalez or Alexander Calder, as well as Picasso's celebrated "Guernica," which was painted for this occasion.[16] Nor was the effort to integrate the arts limited to Europe. In the United States, through initiatives such as the Works Progress Administration (WPA), artists who were later to become well known as members of the New York School participated in public art projects. The Mexican artist Diego Rivera executed large murals, a first one for the Detroit Institute of Fine Arts in 1932, which was criticized as irreligious, and another more famous still, his "Man at the Crossroads," for the Rockefeller Center in New York. The presence of a portrait of Lenin in this work led to its removal and eventual reconstitution at the Palace of Fine Arts in Mexico City.

It may be that the so-called International Style, which called for an architecture devoid of "ornament," and the frenzied pace of post-War construction led to earlier efforts to integrate the arts being abandoned. It should be said that art too, having shifted its center of gravity after the war from Paris to New York, lost its will to participate in anything other than its own aggrandizement. This was to be the time of "art for art's sake," when individual painters and sculptors would execute works that no longer required a patron or a government to support them. The art market in its contemporary version developed a thirst not for murals or paintings made to be in a given place, but for readily movable pieces, at home in a living room or a museum.

More recently, recession and a certain sense that art had reached the limits of its alternative tendencies toward provocation and minimalism, have led numerous artists to strike out into three dimensions and to create works that certainly recall architecture. From the other perspective, that of the architects, the search for alternatives to orthodox Modernism and superficial Post-Modernism has led many to look toward art for inspiration. Then too, the rallying call of many architects has been for their work, once again, as in the past, to be considered art in and of itself. A number of examples, drawn from Europe, the United States and Japan, show just how art and architecture have been drawn together to the point where the distinction between them often blurs.

Pages 146/147
Christo & Jeanne-Claude
Wrapped Reichstag
Berlin, Germany, 1971–95
© Christo 1995
Photo: Wolfgang Volz
These views give not only an idea of the spectacular presence of the Wrapped Reichstag, which most certainly is a work situated at the limits between art and architecture and history, but also make it clear to what an extent the public reacted to this monumental presence in their midst. For the Christos, a major part of the art involved was obtaining the necessary authorizations, and organizing the substantial amount of work necessary for the wrapping of this voluntarily temporary piece.

Europe: Building Art

A number of artists have specifically sought, through installations and other less ephemeral works, to occupy spaces in the urban environment. Such is the case of the French artist Daniel Buren, who is best known for his works made with striped cloth. One intervention of his, ordered by Jack Lang, in the inner courtyard of the Palais Royal in Paris, in front of the Ministry of Culture was highly controversial. Parisians, especially those who were not sympathetic to the Socialists, found his black and white striped columns intolerable in this historic environment. Contested much less, his recent intervention on the Place des Terreaux in Lyon occupies the space of this centrally located square with a geometric pattern of fountains. Though Buren makes no pretense here to create architecture, he does enter into a dialogue with the environment, including the Musée des Beaux Arts and the rear of the city hall, both of which are historic monuments. Just down the street is Jean Nouvel's opera house, which was made by hollowing out the original Lyon Opera house, built by Chenavard and Pollet in 1831. Jean Nouvel managed to triple the interior volume of the structure by digging below, but also by adding a sculptural 20 m high semi-cylindrical drum to the top, which is used for the practice areas of the opera ballet company. These interventions, one more oriented toward architecture and the other toward art, create a meeting place for the two in an old European city center, which is itself an accomplishment.

Christo & Jeanne-Claude are well known for their wrapping of various objects, including the Pont Neuf in Paris. But their most difficult and most architectural work was certainly the 1995 "Wrapped Reichstag," in Berlin. Obviously, the complex history of this building and its central place in the German psyche, together with the decision that it would once again become the seat of the Bundestag, made the Christos' project all the more controversial. A shroud, even a silver one, may have brought forth memories both within Germany and abroad about the past and the future of Berlin. Although temporary, this skin of cloth illustrates the potential for meaningful symbiosis between art and architecture.

One very active architect who has attempted to confront the questions posed by the relationship between art and architecture is the Italian Massimiliano Fuksas. The results of his investigation can be seen in the recent Niaux Cave Entrance, and

Pages 148/149
Daniel Buren
Place des Terreaux
Lyon, France, 1994
After having caused considerable controversy in the early 1980s with his column-studded design for the inner courtyard of the Palais Royal in Paris, Buren took on the equally symbolic Place des Terreaux in Lyon, opposite the Musée des Beaux-Arts and behind the Mairie with its fountain by Bartholdi. Beneath the square, a parking lot was decorated by the artist Matt Mulligan.

Bordeaux Art School. "I believe that the more contemporary architecture goes forward, the more it resembles sculpture," says Fuksas. "In any case," he continues, "the influence of art on architecture is much greater today than it was in the 1970s for example." What sort of art does an architect like Massimiliano Fuksas look toward? "Personally," he answers, "I am interested in Joseph Beuys because of the very strong moral sense of the social usefulness of art which he defended." The example of Beuys, whose influence was felt most over twenty years ago, seems to indicate a certain time gap between art and architecture. "Architects are definitely behind the times," says Fuksas. "As the International Style was emptied of its substance in the 1940s and 1950s, we lost a lot of time," he continues. "It was only in the late 1970s that the first efforts were made to recreate new links between the different types of artistic expression including architecture." When asked how architects and artists have been brought closer together in recent years, Fuksas replies, "Before, architects considered that they should have very little to do with day-to-day life. They were there to give their judgments, to tell others how to live. Today, you would have to be a fool to have such an attitude. But that discovery in itself means that artists and architects have become much more important because they are once again in direct contact with the way people live."[17]

Just as architects have been drawn toward art, the reverse process has also occurred. A case in point is that of the artist Ilya Kabakov, born in Dniepropetrovsk in the Soviet Union in 1933. His monumental installation at the Centre Georges Pompidou in 1995 was entitled "C'est ici que nous vivons" (This is where we live). His own description of this work suffices to give an idea of just how it is related to

Page 151
Massimiliano Fuksas
Entrance to Grotto
Niaux, France, 1988–93
Intended as the public entrance to
a cave containing ancient paintings and inscriptions, this structure in Corten steel with its gates
like the spreading wings or rearing
head of a prehistoric creature is
once again situated at the limit
between sculpture and architecture. Given the context, the architect also attempted here to create
an object that in itself carried a
relationship to archeology: hence
the choice of pre-rusted metal.

Enric Miralles
Unazuki Meditation Center
Toyama, Japan, 1993–94

The undulating tubular presence
of this observation platform
brings it closer to sculpture than
any other work by this talented
Spanish architect. Making reference not only to contemporary
art, but also, and above all to its
natural setting, the platform in

a sense recalls the exuberent
metalwork creations of Antoni
Gaudí. In any case, this example
shows to what an extent contemporary architects are exploring
the limits between art and the art
of building.

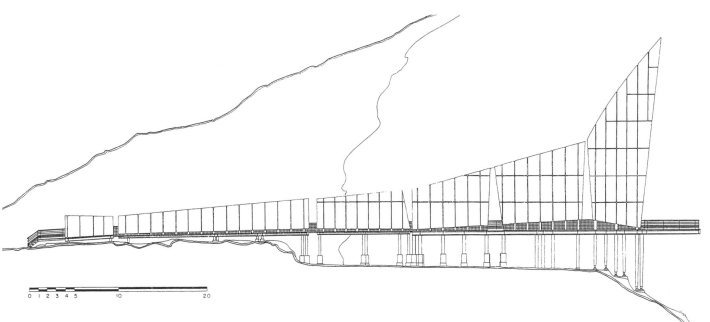

0 1 2 3 4 5   10   20

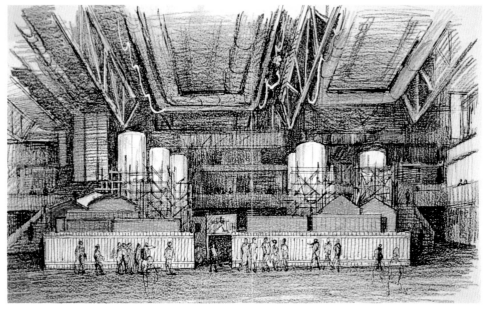

Ilya Kabakov
"C'est ici que nous vivons"
(This is where we live)
Centre Georges Pompidou, Paris,
France, 1995
Like other works by this artist,
who is very much a product of
the former Soviet Union, this
installation was directly related
to architecture in the sense that it
represented "the work site of an
enormous building, probably a
magnificent Palace of the Future."
Abandoned like so many other
dreams, the site of the palace
has become a miserable home
for squatters.

Jean-Pierre Raynaud
"Human Space"
Museum Ludwig, Cologne,
Germany, 1995
In this work, ordered by Peter
Ludwig for the Cologne Museum,
Raynaud has used one of his
favorite motifs, a death's head
or skull, repeated hundreds of
times within the annular structure
that he designed. Through its
occupation of space and its
geometric form, "Human Space"
explores the conventions of
architecture, and in particular
religious buildings.

architecture: "The installation represents the work site of an enormous building, probably a magnificent Palace of the Future. The bases of five enormous columns surrounded by scaffolding are visible. Below, construction materials of various kinds are piled... and in the middle of the site, there is a panel showing what a remarkable place the completed Palace and the city around it will be... But by looking carefully, the visitor will notice that the work here stopped long ago, and that everything has been abandoned. The scaffolding and the construction materials are only a huge waste heap... What was supposed to be a radiant future became the hopeless present, and no one seems to know where to go.[18] Though Kabakov's apocalyptic vision is related to the specific problems of the ex-Soviet Union, his commentary is nonetheless valid for many other grandiose architectural plans. The sense of disorder that he brings to his work also permeates the thinking of architects such as Steven Holl, who seeks to embrace the fundamentally ephemeral nature of urban buildings.

Moving once again to the perspective of an architect who creates in a sculptural mode, the Unazuki Meditation Center, in Toyama, Japan (1991–93) by Barcelona-based Enric Miralles is certainly striking. According to the architect, "A bridge, a small park and an old pilgrim's path are unified and attuned to each other to form this ensemble, experienced as a union with the rugged beauty of nature."[19] A surprising arabesque of steel tubes encircles a viewing platform, integrating architecture and site-specific art into a convincing whole.

Dominique Perrault, the young French architect responsible for the vast new Bibliothèque nationale de France, in Paris, makes clear his own interest in art. "The architecture of the library represents an attempt to create a work which is of its time. The art movements which I look to for inspiration are Land Art or Minimalism. I would have like to have shown this building to Donald Judd before he died. Richard Serra did visit it, and he was extremely favorable in his comments. In my opinion, it is high time for architecture to assimilate the art of our time," says Perrault. When

Pages 154/155
Jean-Pierre Raynaud
"La Mastaba"
La Garenne-Colombes, France,
1988–90
Located in a working class suburb of Paris, this highly unusual structure is neither the home of the artist, nor his atelier. It is a kind of private gallery where few outsiders are admitted. Within, in an underground room (visible to the right), he places works of his own in juxtaposition, to see how they "react" to each other. Inspired by funerary designs, it is entirely clad in white tiles.

asked why he feels that art movements that reached their high point twenty years ago or more should be looked to for inspiration, Dominique Perrault responds, "Twenty years is just about the gap in time which exists between art and architecture."[20]

The French artist Jean-Pierre Raynaud often creates artistic environments that call on a refined sense of architecture, such as "Human Space," a piece created in 1995, for the Ludwig Museum in Cologne. Raynaud has gone a step beyond this reference to the built environment in the Paris suburb of La Garenne-Colombes, where he created a structure that he calls "La Mastaba." Neither a home, nor a private museum, it is rather a space for the contemplation of his own art. The blank exterior walls are covered in his favorite white tiles, and the shape of the building, together with this immaculate cladding, makes for an incongruous presence in a fundamentally working class neighborhood. Although Jean-Pierre Raynaud worked with the architect Jean Dedieu to build this highly unusual structure, its conception is his. Here, one takes a narrow staircase that leads below grade. Both the form of the mastaba and this stairway going into the earth bring forth references to ancient funerary architecture, which the artist does not reject, despite his thoroughly modern approach to art. This is a space of communion with art, and certainly with the prospect of death. Though the first function is readily assumed in much contemporary architecture, the second is usually avoided, although it is one of the great themes of the architecture of the past. It seems that it was necessary for an artist to build a structure so that architecture could find some of its own profound contact with the past, while remaining a witness to the present.

Just as art may enrich new forms in architecture, so furniture and interior design sometimes play their role. Another well-known figure in France, Philippe Starck, recently created the Felix Restaurant in the Peninsula Hotel, Hong Kong. Though this is, strictly speaking, an interior design, it does make a case for the very type of curving unusual forms that Starck has translated into built form on occasion, especially in Japan. The idea that furniture and other objects can take on unusual new shapes certainly has a bearing on the creative trends in architecture, as Starck, Mendini and others have proved.

Finally, an example of the work of an architect that verges on the sculptural should be cited here. Bernard Tschumi's La Villette Follies, on the northern periphery of Paris, challenge the barriers that exist between art and architecture. Usually, it is said that architecture must serve a function, whereas art may be devoid of such practical concerns. Tschumi's follies, emblematic works of the Deconstructivist movement, do occasionally actually serve a purpose (ticket office, café or Red Cross station), but just as often they are decorative objects that give a geometric pattern to the vast Villette park area.

Page 157
Philippe Starck
Felix Restaurant
Peninsula Hotel, Hong Kong, 1995
Situated on the thirtieth floor of one of the finest hotels of Hong Kong, this small 165 m² space includes a 100-seat restaurant, two bars and a minuscule discothèque. Starck's sense of the use of space has led him to cross the barrier between design and architecture, building his own structures, most notably in Japan.

Architect/Artists and Artist/Architects

Frank O. Gehry's thoughts about the inspirational nature of contemporary art have already been quoted in this volume. Two examples of his work, both located in Venice, California, give an idea of how he integrates art and goes on to create his own kind of sculptural work. The most notable feature of the Chiat/Day Main Street building (1986–91) is the central part of the facade, formed by an enormous pair of binoculars designed by Gehry's friends Claes Oldenburg and Coosje van Bruggen. The distinction between art and architecture is further blurred here by the fact that cars enter the structure by passing beneath and through the binoculars. Furthermore, small office or conference spaces have been created within the binocular cylinders.

Gehry's Norton House (1982–84) is a three-story residence built on a narrow beach-front lot facing the Venice boardwalk. It reflects the chaotic architecture of its environment, and calls on such varied materials as concrete block, glazed tile, stucco and wooden logs. Its most notable feature is a freestanding study modeled on the lifeguard stations that dot the wide beaches of Venice and Santa Monica. Just a few meters from this house, California blondes, roller skaters, muscle builders, homeless people and tee-shirt venders jostle each other for attention, and the extraordinary vista toward the Pacific opens. In this very particular and ephemeral environment, Gehry has created a house that responds in an original way, and breaks the usual molds of contemporary architecture. It is, in almost every definable sense, a work of art in itself, calling on the popular culture sources that in fact inspire much contemporary painting or sculpture.

"Two-Way Mirror Cylinder Inside Cube" is a work created by the artist Dan Graham for the Dia Center for the Arts in New York in 1991. This was one of the projects chosen for Terry Riley's 1995 "Light Construction" exhibition at the Museum of Modern Art. As curator Terry Riley writes, "Graham's Two-Way Mirror Cylinder inside Cube, a work which clearly occupies a position 'in between,' consciously refers to the history of glass architecture... But Graham's work... transcends a purely esthetic approach. By incorporating it into his Rooftop Urban Park Project, which he characterizes as a 'utopian presence' in the city, he elevates the work from the status of mere formal abstraction. His contemporary urban park – which, like its traditional counterparts, seeks to reintegrate alienated city dwellers with their environment while providing a contemplative place apart – restores the aesthetic dimension of the glass dream and points toward the idealism that sustained it."[21] The "in between" referred to by Terry Riley is naturally the situation of a work that is between art and architecture, a status that seems to be more and more frequent both in the work of artists and in that of architects.

One of the seminal figures of contemporary art, occupying a unique position as a British exile living in Los Angeles, David Hockney projects his ideas of imaginary space, often expressed in his opera decors, into the shapes of his canvases. A visitor to his Hollywood Hills residence, at the end of a winding road far above the broad boulevards of Los Angeles itself, immediately grasps that his plan is nothing other than to have the vivid colors of his imagination spill out into the "real" world. With his painter's eye, he has transformed his own house into a three-dimensional painting, choosing colors rarely if ever seen in such juxtaposition elsewhere but in his canvases. In works like his recent "Double Entrance" (oil on 2 canvases, 183 x 427 cm, 1995), Hockney explores what he terms "imaginary" space, seeking to go beyond the experiments in this direction of the cubist artists. Fundamentally, such investigation of the very nature of space is precisely the kind of art that should and most probably will have a direct influence on the thinking of architects. There is no longer an unwritten law of construction that provides that only rectilinear structures can be erected in an economically reasonable fashion. Computer-aided design and advances in production methods clearly make it possible to build almost any

Frank O. Gehry
Chiat/Day Main Street
Venice, California, 1986–91
Gehry's friends Claes Oldenburg
and Coosje van Bruggen collaborated on this project, located
on the main road between
Santa Monica and Venice. Their
contribution was of course the
enor-mous pair of binoculars,
which contains office space. Cars
enter the underground parking
lot in the space between the two
"lenses" of the binoculars.

Page 161
**Dan Graham
"Two-Way Mirror Cylinder
Inside Cube"
Dia Center for the Arts, New York,
New York, 1981/91**
Situated on a Manhattan rooftop,
this thoroughly ambiguous work
makes use of reflections and
transparency to mirror and deform
the heterogeneous architectural
environment. It is at once neutral
and critical, present and absent.
As such, it explores themes
that are of considerable interest
to contemporary architects,
particular those of the
"neo-modern" school.

Above
**Frank O. Gehry
Norton House
Venice, California, 1982–84**
This is the quintessential Gehry
house, located a few steps away
from the wide beaches of Venice,
calling not only on the popular
imagery of the local lifeguard
shelters that dot the beach, but
also on a sculptural variety of
unusual materials. Thanks to
Gehry and others, Venice contains
one of the more interesting
collections of small experimental
contemporary buildings to be
seen anywhere in the world.

shape that an architect or an artist can imagine, so why not a vividly colored maelstrom of shapes? The task of the architect would be to make such space livable while affirming the power of art to break existing molds.

One woman who has consistently challenged the barriers that exist between the art world and architecture is Maya Lin. Now thirty-six years old, she was only twenty-one, an architectural student at Yale, when she submitted the winning design for the Vietnam Veterans Memorial in Washington. This V-shaped wedge of black granite is cut into the earth of the Mall, not far from the Washington Monument. On it, in the order of their death, are inscribed the names of the 57,000 Americans who lost their lives in Vietnam. The London daily *The Independent* called Maya Lin's work "the greatest of all modern monuments ... this relentless stretch of lustrous black granite that recalls the name of every poor Jack who died need-

lessly fighting for a political concept – the domino theory – that existed openly in the minds of paranoid, vote-conscious politicians. When you see grown men, who have coursed the heart of darkness in order to indulge the whim of a social elite, trace out the incised names of their comrades, beat Lin's walls with their fists and cry hot tears, you feel instinctively why so many monuments mean nothing to most ordinary people."[22]

It was after designing this seminal monument, visited by more than 2.5 million people each year, that Maya Lin went to graduate school to become an architect. There she encountered one professor who was to have a considerable influence on her. "Frank O. Gehry was very supportive when I was in graduate school," she says. "Frank was a teacher, and when I told him that instead of drawing up a design I wanted to collaborate with a sculptor and build something, he said, 'Great, go ahead.' So, without planning, we built this huge tree house 40 or 50 feet off the forest floor in Vermont. Frank was wonderful. He made me realize that it was OK to be in between art and architecture. I remember him saying, 'Don't worry about the distinctions. Do what you need to do.'"

Today, Maya Lin has worked as an architect in a more traditional sense, building two houses, but she continues to create sculptures as well. When asked if she is making a conscious effort to challenge the barriers between the two disciplines, she answers, "I have not tried to make an overt statement. There is inspiration and artistry involved in making a monument or designing a house, and yet you are still apparently involved in making something which is functional. For me the Vietnam Memorial was a sort of exercise, because I never expected it to be built. It was an ideological commentary about trying to go against our standard approach in the United States to monuments. I tried to avoid making any overt political statement, however. What I was concerned with was not modern art – it was not necessarily an esthetic statement. To be apolitical became political – to not declare a victory. The identification of the individual as the individual – that is a twentieth century idea. I had no notion of making a hybrid of earthworks of the 1970s and architecture. I do not tend to approach that kind of esthetic theorizing or commentary within the work. I leave it to others to make such comments."[23]

The architect Michael Rotondi, one of the founders of the SCI-Arc school in Santa Monica, and former partner of Thom Mayne in the firm Morphosis, has created a new firm with Clark Stevens. Called RoTo, this firm has worked on a number of highly unusual projects, which challenge accepted ideas about the materials and forms of architecture. Their Gemini Learning Center, in Morristown, New Jersey, was designed for an international business consulting group. It is intended to

David Hockney Residence
Hollywood Hills, California
Photographed in 1994
Like many of his works of art, the home of David Hockney is painted in the saturated colors that he prefers. The intensity and presence of these colors is such that the visitor has the impression of entering a painting, an idea that Hockney obviously encourages.

David Hockney
"Double Entrance"
Oil on 2 canvases
183 x 427 cm, 1995
David Hockney maintains that Cubist art opened certain ideas of space that were not fully explored by its inventors. He has taken it upon himself to go further, creating what he calls "imaginary space," a kind of dream world whose colors are inspired by the brightness of southern California. Though he has created numerous decors for operas, the artist has expressed the hope to create a walk-in environment with works of this type.

develop "new ideas and ways of thinking about the world and its social-economic structure." According to the firm, "The architectural concepts were framed and shaped by the terms collaboration, dynamical systems and structures, and trans-formative processes." The idea of including pieces of natural tree trunks in the design is part of a "growth" theme given to the interior, which includes a carpet the color of a forest floor, and piles of "rocks." These elements, together with the "folded walls" made of plywood fastened to welded steel frames at unusual angles, give the project a sculptural aspect, at a time when much contemporary sculpture and installation art calls in a similar fashion on a variety of unusual materials.

Josh Schweitzer's Monument (1987–90), located in Joshua Tree, California, comes as close to sculpture as functional architecture can. The Joshua Tree National Monument is a desert area located three hours by car outside of Los Angeles. This small (90 m²) house, intended for the use of the architect and five friends, is located on a 4 ha site within the confines of the park. It is an assemblage of one-room build-ings, each containing a separate function. There is an orange, porch-like structure that is a shaded outdoor space. The olive-green pavilion contains a 3.5 m high living room, while a purple-blue volume contains a dining area, kitchen and sleeping spaces. Built with painted stucco walls, exposed aggregate concrete floors and windows framed with redwood, The Monument is a homage to its surroundings, imbued with a "monastic solemnity." As the architect says, "Its colors are the colors of the desert." He also cites Rudolph Schindler's ideal of the house as a "permanent camp" as an inspiration for this structure.

Occasionally, a close working relationship between an architect and an artist brings new light to the differences and similarities between the disciplines. Richard Meier and Frank Stella have known each other and worked together since the 1950s. In recent years, Stella has explored the idea of actually creating architecture, for example in the case of the pavilion of the Groninger Museum, which was finally built by Coop Himmelblau. Then too, there is a very definite sense of an architec-tural, if imaginary, space in much of his work ("Hooloomooloo 1,2,3," 1994, triptych, 1: 340 x 299 cm; 2: 340 x 630 cm; 3: 340 x 254 cm; "Watson and the Shark," 1995, aluminum on iron base. Overall: 151 x 192 x 138 cm). Richard Meier has engaged in the opposite form of exploration, creating both collages and his own sculpture, which bears more than a passing resemblance to that of Stella ("Saulgau," 1994, 38 x 67 x 71 cm, sculpture). When asked if he feels that there is a blurring of

the lines between art and architecture, Richard Meier replies, "No. I'm not sure there's so much of the blurring of the lines. I think it's simply that more artists want to be architects. Maybe historically more architects have wanted to be artists, but I think that today more and more artists really would like to make architecture. Frank Stella is a good example, and a number of projects which he has made in Europe are for buildings, and in a sense incorporated in the conception of those buildings is the artist's view. I think that the beginning points are usually different for an artist than an architect. The artist has an idea of what might be, and then finds someone who wants that idea. Generally an architect waits for someone to come to him with a project and then says, 'I have an idea for what you can do.'" As Richard Meier says, he draws a line "between the architecture of artists and the architecture of architects," but he does not hesitate to call his own Frankfurt Museum of Decorative Arts "a work of art." "I consider that most of my buildings are works of art," he says, "but I have observed a number of artists who are trying to do architecture. On the surface, one would say that could be by an architect, or could be by an artist, but I believe that the approach of the artist is fundamentally different from that of the architect. As an architect you have built-in judgments about entry, about accessibility, about movement, about how a structure might be inhabited, rather than being simply concerned about the form and relationship of the construction, or constructional elements."[24]

Right
RoT<u>o</u>
Gemini Learning Center
Morristown, New Jersey, 1995
Used by the Gemini Consulting firm to train business people to react rapidly in the current changeable environment, this facility, contained within a 1960s office building, is intended to reflect a theme of "metamorphosis and three-dimensional thinking." The screen made of tree trunks (right) is intended to provide a certain privacy without creating isolation.

Page 164
Maya Lin
Vietnam Veterans Memorial
Washington, D.C., 1981–83
Designed at a time when the Post-Modern style was all the rage in America, the sober power of Maya Lin's black granite wedge, gouged into the earth of the Mall, remains a powerful symbol to all of those who lost relatives in the Vietnam war. With its 57,000 names, engraved in the order of their death, the monument takes on a poignant humanity that so often is lacking in modern design and architecture.

A younger architect, Simon Ungers, born in Cologne, Germany in 1957, approached his client's desire for a combined house and library by creating the T-House, which has been rightfully compared to a sculpture by Richard Serra. The weathering steel used by Ungers certainly brings to mind Serra's preferred Corten steel. Ungers has actually completed more works of installation art than he has buildings. Tellingly, he compares his T-House (designed with Tom Kinslow) to a sculpture he created with structural steel at Hunter's Point in New York, or with a 1993 work he called "Red Slab in Space." As he says about the latter work, "Red Slab in Space is a monolithic, monochrome construction that integrates the two existing columns of the gallery space and uses them structurally. It is a synthesis of painting, sculpture and architecture, and attempts to establish a connection to early Modernism, in particular Constructivism, De Stijl and Purism, which sought a similar integration. The same could also be said of the T-House."

A final interesting case of symbiosis between architecture and art is the work of Lebbeus Woods. His complex, apocalyptic drawings for buildings that most often will never be built have had a considerable influence on architectural thinking. He has participated in several projects organized by Peter Noever, Director of the Österreichisches Museum für Angewandte Kunst in Vienna. The most recent of these, the International Conference on Contemporary Architecture, held in Havana,

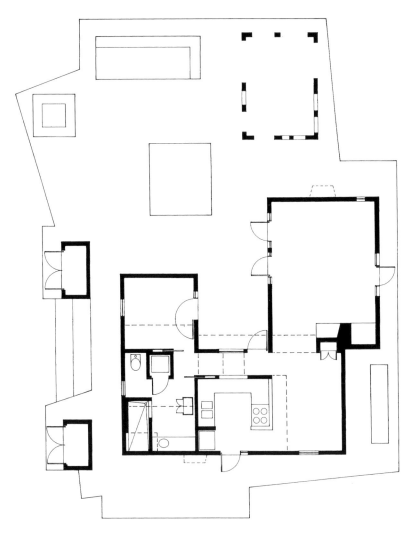

Pages 166/167
Schweitzer BIM
The Monument
Joshua Tree, California, 1987–90
Located just outside the Joshua
Tree National Monument, this
90 m² house is designed to fit into
its spectacular natural environment. "The colors," says the
architect Josh Schweitzer, "are
the colors of the desert," and
"the monolithic forms of the
buildings echo the forms of the
rocks." This house approaches
art as much as any functional
structure can.

Cuba, in January 1995 gave rise to his Havana Project, which is a proposal for a dynamic reassessment of the architectural needs of this city. The drawings of Lebbeus Woods, together with proposals on the same theme by Coop Himmelblau, Zaha Hadid, Steven Holl, Thom Mayne, Eric Owen Moss, and Carme Pinós, were conceived for an exhibition whose theme would be the movement toward "architecture that comprises complexity, sensitivity, and dynamics; architecture that focuses on the human being and withstands commercial definitions; architecture that copes with new tasks as well as the old traditional ones – an everyday architecture that yet contains the claim of universality and topicality – architecture as a universal and unifying metaphor of space, time and body." Although the participants in this conference were all architects, they are also architects who tend toward an artistic vision of their work. The movement of art and architecture toward each other seems both inevitable and fruitful.

Above
Frank Stella
"Hooloomooloo 1,2,3"
Triptych, 1 : 340 x 299 cm;
2 : 340 x 630 cm; 3 : 340 x 254 cm,
1994
Many of the recent works of Frank Stella are derived from his experimentation with the manipulation on a computer of forms such as those of smoke rings. Although his architectural projects, such as the wing of the Groninger Museum, which was eventually built by Coop Himmelblau, have not come to fruition, it is obvious that he maintains a substantial interest in the point of juncture between two and three dimensions in his art.

Right
Frank Stella
"Watson and the Shark"
Aluminum on iron base
Overall : 151 x 192 x 138 cm, 1995
Many of Frank Stella's paintings
are three-dimensional though,
they still hang on walls. In more
recent years, he has experimented
with pure sculpture, which takes
on the very complex forms that
seem to be latent in his computer-
related paintings. In his mind,
the next logical step would be to
translate his ideas into the larger
three-dimensional environment
of architecture.

Pages 170/171
Simon Ungers and Tom Kinslow
T-House
Wilton, New York, 1988–94
Built on an 18 ha plot of forested
land, the T-House is related
in its design to installation art
created by Simon Ungers.
Monolithic in appearance and
design, the structure is built
with 1/4 inch oxidized nickel
chromium steel, which certainly
emphasizes its overtly sculptural
character. The simple geometric
form is derived from the
client's desire to separate the
living quarters (below) from the
library (above).

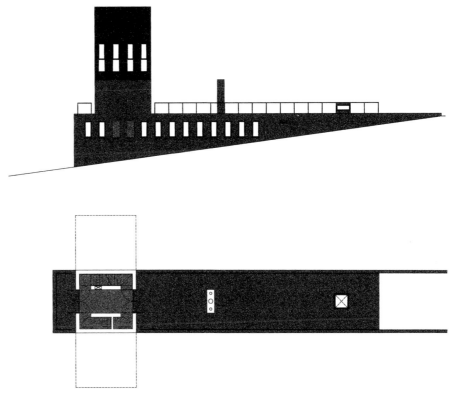

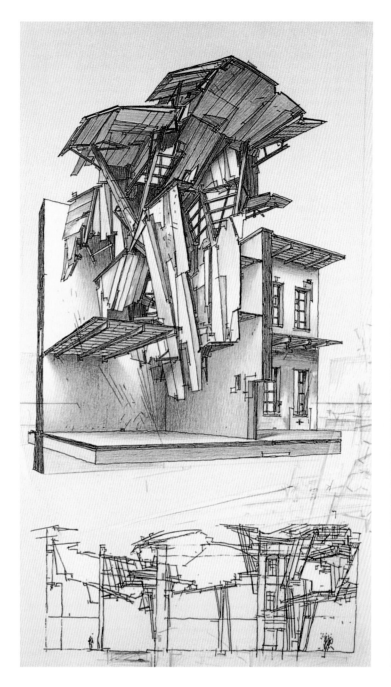

Lebbeus Woods
Havana Project
Havana, Cuba, 1995 (project)

Lebbeus Woods has participated in several projects organized by Peter Noever, Director of the Österreichisches Museum für Angewandte Kunst in Vienna. The most recent of these, the International Conference on Contemporary Architecture, held in Havana, Cuba, in January 1995, gave rise to his Havana Project, which is a proposal for a dynamic reassessment of the architectural needs of this city.

Tadashi Kawamata
Roosevelt Island Project
New York, New York, 1992
Kawamata has obtained a considerable international reputation by creating ephemeral environments made of mostly reused wood. His use of the word "cancer" to describe the way in which these works seem to be excreted by the buildings that they are attached to is revealing. They are certainly a commentary on precarious living conditions, and are difficult to classify as either sculpture or architecture.

Japan: The Ceremonial Way

In Japan, too, there have been numerous efforts to bring different art forms into closer contact. The Japanese context is of course a very particular one, because of the strong role played by tradition. That tradition, whether it be in terms of the visualization of space or of the use of materials, does not seem as distant from contemporary creation as is Western tradition. That fact undoubtedly explains the wealth of creators working at the boundaries between disciplines. One case in point is Tadashi Kawamata. Born in 1953 on the northern island of Hokkaido, he studied to be a painter, but found that he was more fascinated by the demolition and reconstruction of a building visible from his window. "From my window," he says, "I was a witness to the operation of the urban metabolism, a digestion and regurgitation of materials which are linked to the life cycle of the city." From that moment on, Kawamata created increasingly complex wooden environments, at documenta 8 (1987), in Toronto (1989) and in other cities around the world. His most ambitious construction, his Roosevelt Island Project, was built and demolished in New York between August and December 1992 in an abandoned hospital. Revealingly, Kawamata uses the word "cancer" to describe his own work. Indeed, his chaotic scaffolding/sculptures are always an outgrowth of existing, often abandoned buildings. His works are ephemeral, as are indeed most urban structures, and they call attention to the idea of the city as a living organism. Perhaps closer to the shanty towns that surround many third world cities than to the gleaming new forms conceived by many architects, Kawamata's works, made from reused wood, also recall that the most widely spread forms of construction in the world are indeed of such spontaneous nature.

Although Kawamata vigorously rejects any relationship between his use of wood and the animist traditions of Japan, it is a fact that much Japanese art and architecture is fashioned from wood. Another important artist who works principally with bamboo is Hiroshi Teshigahara. Director of the famous Sogetsu ikebana school in Tokyo, he is the son of Sofu Teshigahara, who was responsible, together with Kenzo Tange, for a return to interest in Japanese cultural traditions after the rejection that followed World War II. Hiroshi Teshigahara creates environments out of bamboo, which resemble a kind of traditionally inspired installation art. In 1992 and 1993, he created an installation for the traditional Japanese tea ceremony, at Numazu, a former residence of the Emperor 100 km to the southwest of Tokyo. Pavilions for the tea ceremony were designed here by Tadao Ando, Arata Isozaki and Kiyonori Kikutake. A slightly different version of his installation was seen in 1993 at Unesco, in Paris. Like the great master of the tea ceremony Sen no Rikyo (1521–91), the ambition of Teshigahara here would appear to be the creation of a total work of art, in which installation, garden and architecture participate in a unified expression.

For certain figures, it seems obvious that a blending of different types of artistic expression is inevitable. The great Japanese couturier Issey Miyake is one of these creators. His work has frequently been shown in museums of art, and it is no coincidence that he is a close friend of architects like Isozaki and Ando. In his global approach to fashion, there is an undeniable architectural element, which can already be seen in his development of unusual textiles.

The analysis of space and volume implicit in architecture can clearly be influenced in certain instances by the new vision brought to these subjects by artists. Contrary to a widely held opinion, Japan has counted a number of highly important

Isamu Noguchi
Noguchi Atelier
Mure, Awajishima, Japan
Photographed in 1994
Noguchi's magnificent atelier in Mure is unfortunately not open to the public, but it contains many of his late works, which are carefully selected pieces of stone that he has only slightly retouched, drilling a hole through them or scoring a deep line along one surface. Admired by architects like Arata Isozaki, Tadao Ando and I.M. Pei, Noguchi had a very pronounced awareness of architectural space.

artists in the post-war years. Some of these have not been recognized in the West because of the direct connection of their work to Japanese tradition. Others may have been underestimated. Such would seem to be the case of the sculptor Isamu Noguchi (1904–88), born of a Japanese father and an American mother. Noguchi's last studio, located in the town of Mure, on the island of Shikoku, is unfortunately not open to the public because of legal disputes. Hundreds of his sculptures, often looking like massive blocks of unsculpted stone, are piled and placed in the grounds of this property. Noguchi is of interest to the debate about the relationship between art and architecture because of his masterful sense of space. He brought a Japanese sense of minimal intervention, a kind of Zen spirit to contemporary art, and showed that space and form could be seen in a different way, while keeping their deep, intimate connection to the past, and indeed to nature. Again, it will come as no surprise that members of the Japanese committee for the defense of Noguchi's work include Ando, Isozaki and Miyake.

Japan's cities, Tokyo foremost among them, are not at all similar to their Western counterparts. The massive, sprawling vista of urban Tokyo is enough to impress even the most blasé of visitors. More often than not, Tokyo seems to new visitors to be a pure expression of chaos – even neighboring buildings can face in different directions as though intent on breaking rank and going their own way. But there are reasons for this, and apparent chaos may indeed be a different, or higher, form of organization. A German artist, Raffael Rheinsberg, born in 1943 in Kiel, seems to have captured this in his piece "Another World, Another Time," installed in 1993 at the Kamakura Museum. Made with electronic components, this large work suggests that what looks disorganized may indeed be highly sophisticated, a lesson that some contemporary architects seem to have absorbed in recent years.

Three architects, two of them foreigners, have brought different approaches to a new relationship between art and architecture in Japan. I.M. Pei's 1990 Bell Tower at Misono, Shiga, for example is based in its form on a traditional Japanese musical instrument, the *bachi*. Built for a religious sect near Kyoto, this bell tower is one of Pei's purest and most spiritual structures.

Much less spiritual, the buildings of Shin Takamatsu, such as his Syntax located in Kyoto, are often based on an exaggerated machine metaphor. Takamatsu's drawings, though, give an eerie presence to forms that are often anthropomorphic as well as mechanical.

A final, almost amusing example is that of Philippe Starck's, "La Flamme," built in Tokyo in 1990 for the brewer Asahi. Starck compared this structure to a "black granite urn placed on a luminescent glass stairway, and topped with a golden flame." Indeed the French designer believes that nothing should keep buildings from being designed like objects, a radical idea that has prevented him from working frequently in Europe as an architect. The Japanese, however, for all their respect for tradition, are much more apt to accept such a new concept. The Asahi building is in fact not very successful internally. It functions best as a symbol at the edge of a very busy elevated road, and it does show that different art forms can and do enrich the vocabulary of contemporary architecture.

Shin Takamatsu
Syntax
Kyoto, Japan, 1988–90 (drawing)
At least in the 1980s, Shin Takamatsu achieved a considerable degree of recognition by designing buildings with a robotic or mechanical appearance. Given that the quality of Japanese construction is remarkable, his buildings achieve a kind of artistic perfection, which may not be evident in their aggressive or even comical designs. In the 1990s, Takamatsu has shifted to a more "neo-modern" style.

Right

Philippe Starck

La Flamme

Asahi Breweries, Tokyo, Japan, 1990

Starck says with an impish grin that he is a "creator of monsters." Some of his critics might be tempted to agree with that assessment in front of this surprising "black granite urn placed on a luminescent glass stairway, and topped with a golden flame." The Japanese economic downturn in the 1990s seems to have put a stop to the construction of such eccentric buildings, at least temporarily.

Bottom

I.M. Pei

Bell Tower

Misono, Shiga, Japan, 1992

Located at the end of a curving ceremonial way paved with old stones from the streets of Kyoto, which is located one hour by car from this site, Pei's Bell Tower forms the entrance to a vast open plaza. At the other end of the plaza is located the sanctuary of the Shinji Shumeikai sect, designed by Minoru Yamasaki. Pei is completing a museum for the same sect on a site 1 km from this one.

Shapes for the Future

Page 179
Tadao Ando
Meditation Space, UNESCO
Paris, France, 1994–95
(detail of ceiling)

Concentrating on Europe, the United States and Japan, this survey has attempted to demonstrate that a number of factors have given rise to new forms in architecture in the past ten years. Naturally, the factors that influence architecture, from the economy to the spreading use of computer-aided design, are numerous. Some of these factors, such as the computer, are so powerful that they will continue to transform the shapes and function of architecture at an accelerating pace in the years to come. As John Frazer has written, "A new architecture is being conceived in cyberspace by the global cooperation of a world community evolving new ideas by modeling ecologically responsible environments and using the computer as an evolutionary accelerator. This movement is reinforced culturally by similar thinking in music and other art forms. The emphasis has moved from product to process as Buckminster Fuller, John Cage and Marshall McLuhan all foresaw; and it has moved from forms to the relationship between forms and their users. This paradigm shift will change our understanding and interpretation of past architecture as surely as it will change the way we conceive of the new."[25] It has already been suggested here that the relationship between art and architecture has become closer, and that art has been a source for certain architectural explorations. Most often the published histories of architecture concentrate on the direct, formal and esthetic criteria that influence the built form, but recent trends suggest that a more holistic approach, taking into account such apparently "peripheral" influences as art and the evolution of economic concerns, might permit a better understanding of the contemporary situation. Below, a certain number of built works are highlighted. Some have already been mentioned in this volume, others have not. In principle, each places emphasis on different trends that influence architecture, from the varying approaches to tradition to ecological concerns and formal, artistic ones. The liberty of expression given to architecture in part by computers, but also by the evolving attitudes toward the built form, and new sources of inspiration such as contemporary art, is the subject of this chapter.

Japanese Masters of Light and Space

The Osaka architect Tadao Ando has had a considerable influence on schools of architecture throughout the world. His rigorous approach and his development of a Modernist vocabulary in the context of Japanese tradition certainly make him a figure to be reckoned with for the years to come. What is not always fully appreciated is the almost sensual quality that he gives to his concrete structures. Concrete generally does not photograph well, and the play of light across its surfaces can only really be felt by visiting Ando's buildings in Japan. That said, his recent Meditation Space at the UNESCO headquarters in Paris can give some idea of his accomplishments to Westerners. Squeezed into a very difficult site behind Pier Luigi Nervi's Assembly Hall and next to Marcel Breuer's headquarters building, Ando's structure is a 6.5 m high cylinder made of concrete, with an area of only 33 m². Its floor, like the entrance area of Kisho Kurokawa's Hiroshima Museum of Modern Art, is paved

Page 180
Steven Holl
D.E. Shaw and Company Office
New York, New York, 1991–92
Calling on the phenomenon of "projected color," in which hidden surfaces that are exposed to daylight and painted in saturated colors reflect and diffuse light in space, Steven Holl has given the large cubic entrance of these offices a stunning if somewhat minimal design. This view might bring to mind a cross between Mondrian, Richard Serra and Dan Flavin.

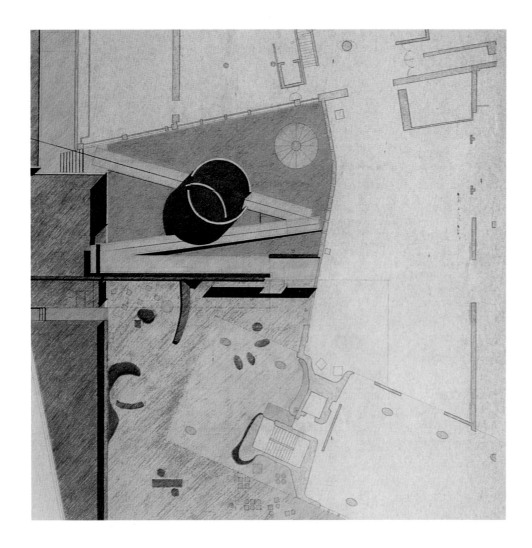

Pages 182/183
Tadao Ando
Meditation Space, UNESCO
Paris, France, 1994–95
This small structure, with a floor area of only 33 m², is located on a 350 m² site squeezed between Marcel Breuer's UNESCO Headquarters (1953–58) and the adjacent Conference Hall designed by Pier Luigi Nervi. Significantly, it is also next to the Japanese garden created by Isamu Noguchi (1956–58) with 88 tons of stone brought from Shikoku. Inside the 6.5 m high concrete cylinder, which has two openings, but no doors, light enters through a narrow strip skylight running around the perimeter.

with granite irradiated by the 1945 bomb. Although not his best work, this Contemplation Space does show that geometric rigor is not antithetical with a non-denominational spirituality, an interesting message in times of trouble.

Since art has become difficult and expensive to collect, many municipalities and prefectures in Japan have turned to alternative ideas. Such is the case of the Museum of Fruit, situated in the Park of Fruits by the Fuefuki River in the Yamanashi Prefecture. According to the architect, Itsuko Hasegawa, "Three structures with differing characteristics are aligned on a shallow southeast slope offering a wonderful view of Mount Fuji. These shelters include a tropical greenhouse, an atrium even space and a building which acts as a workshop for the teaching of hobbies." The unusual shapes of the Museum of Fruit are computer generated. As Hasegawa says, "The geometry of the three shelters was studied through three-dimensional data created on a computer. Each shape was created through the rotation of simple bodies into complex volumes . . . The capability to use such complex forms was made possible only with CAD."[26]

With his Yatsushiro Municipal Museum, and other more recent structures, Toyo Ito has created a place for himself as one of the foremost practitioners of what Rem Koolhaas called a "lite architecture" *(sic).* "While others try to develop an esthetics of disappearance," Koolhaas stated, "Ito effortlessly disappears, while still stimulating events." Ito himself has written about the great similarities he sees between the design of microchips and the evolving patterns of cities, particularly in Japan. He sees the city as a "garden of microchips." "Microchips," he says, "clearly evoke images that are different from those of mechanical objects. These images are not so much of forms as of a space in which invisible things flow. One might describe that space as a transparent field in which diverse phenomenal forms emerge as the result

of flows. What is important here is not so much the expressed forms as the image of a space that makes the expression of those forms possible."[27]

With buildings like his Tokyo Metropolitan Gymnasium, or Tepia, Fumihiko Maki has indeed placed himself in a different realm than a younger architect like Toyo Ito. In Maki's explanations of his own work, there is less reference to the "electronic age" and the forms that it elicits, than there is an effort to look deeper into the built environment. He writes: "We may need to commit ourselves once more to seeing things from the perspective of space. Up to now, our view, our standards, and our norms and process of design with respect to architecture have depended on our looking at (it) from the outside. To look at architecture from the inside naturally means concerning ourselves first of all with the extent of the primary spaces that are required. It is only when we look at architecture from the inside as well as from the outside that we understand how (it) frames and shapes the landscape in addition to standing silhouetted against the landscape."[28]

Like an old radical professor, Kazuo Shinohara, author of the Tokyo Institute of Technology, Centennial Hall, presides over this debate, relating the strengths of Japanese tradition to a broad-minded acceptance of chaos theory and other manifestations of the altogether modern world in which contemporary Japanese must live. It is significant both of Shinohara's analysis and of the Japanese spirit that his earlier works were apparently very traditional houses. A thoughtful application of the lessons of the past to the perceptions of the present by Shinohara and a certain number of other Japanese architects place this country in the vanguard of thought about contemporary design.

One of Shin Takamatsu's most outstanding works is his 1985 Kirin Plaza, located on one of the busiest pedestrian corners of Osaka. Manipulating his machine metaphors, Takamatsu creates an almost unreal point of silent strength, surrounded by the outrageous glowing signs for crab restaurants and cheap movies that are typical of the immediate environment. Takamatsu calls this 50 m high quadruple tower, which emits a gentle white light, a "monument without form." Despite its very modern appearance, this seemingly unnatural calm brings to mind the fact that calm and reflection are traditions of the Japanese spirit, which are being swept aside by rampant urbanization and commercialization.

Pages 184/185
Itsuko Hasegawa
Museum of Fruit
Yamanashi-shi, Yamanashi, Japan, 1993–95
On a generous park site of 195,000 m², with a distant view of Mount Fuji, this group of buildings includes a total floor area of 6,459 m². The museum takes the form of a group of shelters and underground spaces set into sloped ground, each of which accommodates specific programs. It is also a metaphor of a group of seeds, an expression of the fertility and vitality of fruit.

Pages 186/187
Shin Takamatsu
Kirin Plaza
Osaka, Japan, 1985–87

Located in one of the busiest pedestrian intersections of a popular district of Osaka, the Kirin Plaza tower stands out as a calm presence against a chaotic background of extravagant movie posters and signs for local restaurants, which include such remarkable kitsch designs as a giant crab with moving claws. Although very much in the mechanical style of Takamatsu, the tower takes on a solidity conferred in part by its remarkably crafted materials.

American Dreams

Peter Eisenman, once a member of the so-called "New York Five," has been more independent in recent years, creating an international reputation for himself without actually building very much. His Greater Columbus Convention Center, in Columbus, Ohio, does give an idea, however, of the unusual configurations of his designs. Eisenman's case is an interesting one because of his influence on the architectural world, but also because he takes the point of view that it is not the role of the architect to simply make people comfortable by creating attractive buildings. Eisenman's attention to form, though, raises the question whether he too is not privileging esthetics over function.

"I would not say esthetics, but rather formal questions," counters the architect. "Formal questions deal with critical issues. I am looking for ways of conceptualizing space that will place the subject in a displaced relationship because they will have no iconographic references to traditional forms of organization. That is what I have always been trying to do – to oblige the subject to reconceptualize architecture. Ninety percent of architecture is banal, functional-casual. That is why we have to try to make it less casual – to make the reactions of people to architecture less casual. Richard Meier or Michael Graves are still trying to achieve that purpose through image, and I am saying that media has taken over image. We can no longer try to contest the superiority of the media in terms of trying to capture attention. We have to actually change the relationship of the body to architecture. The body has to send messages to the brain saying 'Wait a minute, something that I need to adjust to, something that I need to understand, is happening to me.' It is no longer a question of philosophy or esthetics, and I don't need Jacques Derrida to tell me how to do that. I have also moved away from seeking new forms of organization in known,

Pages 188/189
Peter Eisenman
Greater Columbus
Convention Center
Columbus, Ohio, 1989–93
Obliged to rethink some of the interior spaces of this structure because the client considered them "too radical," Eisenman nonetheless succeeded in creating a highly unusual form for a type of building that usually is very ordinary in appearance. Metal siding of various colors was used to emphasize the layering of the strands of the building, which is located close to the downtown area of the city.

natural phenomena. I like the idea that architecture comes from some sort of molten state in forming itself, rather than starting from a container. We all design architecture from the peripheries in. I am suggesting that we should design from the inside out."[29]

Whatever the shape of Peter Eisenman's built work, he is trying to grapple with issues of meaning in architecture at least for purposes of debate. His counterpart in the world of American architecture is certainly Frank O. Gehry, who has always been much more concerned with the craft of building and the artistic use of often apparently banal materials. His headquarters building for Vitra, in Birsfelden, Switzerland, is a 6,000 m^2 building designed so that the offices can become showrooms. Zoning in the area required a building less than 10 m high, and the Swiss energy code did not allow air-conditioning, so natural ventilation was provided for through windows, and the southern wall was shaded by a large canopy. The main entrance and reception area is located centrally to permit its use in the case of possible future expansion. Plans for the building make it clear that the richer, sculpted space is concentrated around the entrance, ceding to much more rectilinear design elsewhere. The concrete and masonry structure is covered with a combination of painted stucco and zinc metal panels. Although the Vitra entrance area is a remarkable piece of architectural sculpture, it is not clear here that Gehry has done anything more for the building than to create an appealing exterior shape.

His Festival Disney complex in Marne-la-Vallée, outside of Paris, offers a richer vision of his talents. A total of 18,000 m^2 of boutiques and restaurants make up the contents of these buildings. The most visible aspect of the architecture is certainly the series of towers, covered with specially oxidized stainless steel panels, which catch the sunlight during the day and that serve to hold up a web of 3,500 small lights, which illuminate the entire area at night. True to his reputation, Frank O. Gehry has created a series of unique architectural forms, and has used materials as

varied as natural zinc, asphalt, plaster and concrete, often in unexpected combinations. Festival Disney retains something of the Californian charm of Frank O. Gehry's earlier projects, such as his Edgemar Complex in Venice. Partial reuse of an existing structure, and a palette of different, usually inexpensive materials, once again give a sculptural complexity to this work. In many ways, Gehry is the essential pioneer of the search for new architectural forms through an artistic approach. As with much contemporary art though, Gehry's essential source material is popular, even industrial culture, with the apparent banality of asphalt or chain-link fence taking on an esthetic dimension in his hands.

Born in 1929, Frank O. Gehry seems to feel that his time to build "great" works has come. Unfortunately, his Disney Concert Hall in Los Angeles is at least temporarily halted. His Bilbao Museum in Spain is on the other hand advancing rapidly. Located in the center of the cultural district formed by the Museo de Bellas Artes, the University de Deusto, and the Opera House, on a 32,700 m² site formerly occupied by a factory and parking lot, the new Bilbao Museum is scheduled to open in the summer of 1997. Three firms participated in an invited competition, Gehry, Arata Isozaki and Coop Himmelblau, and the groundbreaking took place on October 22, 1993. Designed in a cooperative arrangement with New York's Guggenheim, the museum will have 10,500 m² of galleries, 2,500 m² of public space, with a 50 m high atrium, an auditorium, a museum store, a restaurant, and a café. Project cost for the 24,000 m² building is estimated at $100 million. A sculptural metallic roof form reminiscent of a "metallic flower," designed with the assistance of the CATIA three-dimensional aerospace computer modeling program, unifies the project into a single architectural composition. Building materials are titanium, limestone, and

Pages 190/191
Frank O. Gehry
Vitra Headquarters
Basel, Switzerland, 1992–94
Located in Birsfelden, at the periphery of Basel, this 6,000 m² building is intended as a first phase of a larger development for the same furniture manufacturer who commissioned Gehry to build the Vitra Design Museum and Manufacturing Facility in Weil am Rhein, just across the German border. Aside from the sculptural surfaces of the entrance area visible here, the rest of the building is relatively traditional.

Right
Frank O. Gehry
Edgemar Complex
Venice, California, 1985–87
Located just down the road from
the Chiat/Day Main Street building, built on the site of an ice
cream factory and egg processing
plant, this group of structures
shows all of the diversity and
sculptural inventiveness of Gehry,
calling extensively, for example,
on chain-link fencing material and
varying color and surface effects
to the widest extent possible.
Given its apparently low budget,
this building may not exist in
100 years, but then again, most
of Los Angeles probably won't
either.

Page 192
Frank O. Gehry
Festival Disney
Marne-la-Vallée, France, 1990–92
Inspired by the electrical relay
stations he saw near railroad
stations in the United States,
the stainless steel clad towers of
this large restaurant and boutique
complex hold up a web of tiny
lights, which add to the festive
atmosphere in the evening.
Aside from the signs in the interior
street of the complex, Gehry
imposed his own design on
Disney, no small feat in itself.

glass. The museum's largest space will be a large boat-shaped gallery completely
free of structural columns and measuring 130 m by 30 m. Most gallery ceiling
heights will be 6 m or more, which, together with the spectacular atrium, should
give a very generous feeling of space to the whole.

Perhaps less oriented to the sophisticated manipulation of construction materials than Frank O. Gehry, the New York architect Steven Holl has demonstrated on
numerous occasions that the exploration of light and space in architecture does not
inevitably entail extremely high costs. The offices he completed for D.E. Shaw and
Company in 1991 are located on the top two floors of a skyscraper on 45th Street
between 6th and 7th Avenues. These are offices for a company that makes extensive use of computers for trading, pausing only in the one and a half hour period
when the Tokyo exchange has closed and the London exchange has not yet opened.
Steven Holl's design, which received a 1992 National Honor Award from the
American Institute of Architects, explores color reflection or "projected color."
According to Holl's description, "The metal framing and sheet-rock with skim-coat
plaster was carved and notched at precise points around the central 31 foot cube of

Left
Steven Holl
D.E. Shaw and Company Office
New York, New York, 1991–92
The reception area of this firm,
located in a mid-town New York
high-rise, is a 10 m cube with
minimal furnishing, some of which
was designed by the architect.
With its geometric cutouts, which
use refracted light to introduce
an element of color into the otherwise white environment, this
space is typically one of the
1990s, sparse, with a reminiscence
of the early days of modernism.

space at the entry. Color was applied to the backsides of surfaces, invisible to the
viewer within the space. Natural and artificial lights project this color back into the
space around walls and fissures. As the phenomenon greatly reduces the intensity
of the color being reflected, a range of fluorescent colors could be utilized on the
unseen surfaces, creating a mysterious calm glow." Completed within a $500,000
budget, this project was intended as part of an ongoing expansion.

Philip Johnson has been a central figure of contemporary American architecture
for more than six decades, beginning with his contribution to the 1932 book *The
International Style*, written with Henry-Russell Hitchcock. Just prior to his ninetieth
birthday in 1995, Johnson built a new visitors pavilion on his 20 ha, New Canaan,
Connecticut estate, which includes his famous 1949 Glass House. He calls this building "the Monster," and as *The New York Times* critic Herbert Muschamp has it, he has
"created a bending, rippling, twisting structure with an interior that puts compu-
terized morphs to shame."[30] Made of concrete sprayed on a flexible metal frame,
it is painted in red and black acrylic, and is almost windowless. As surely as any discourse of Peter Eisenman, this building represents a shift in architecture away from
the geometrically defined spaces of the very International Style that Johnson
helped to launch. As Herbert Muschamp points out, appropriate historical references here might be to post-World War I German Expressionist architecture, as in

Page 195
Philip Johnson
Gatehouse
New Canaan, Connecticut, 1995
"The purpose of this building,"
says Philip Johnson, "is to serve as
a reception for tourists to see a
film and wait their turn for the
tour (of the estate) to begin.
The real purpose, however," he
confides, "is to test out my new
theory of architecture without
right angles, without verticals,
made more like a piece of sculpture." Made with prefabricated
panels of structural wire mesh
around an insulating urethane
foam core, cut and bent to
shape and then sprayed with
concrete, the pavilion measures
about 84 m².

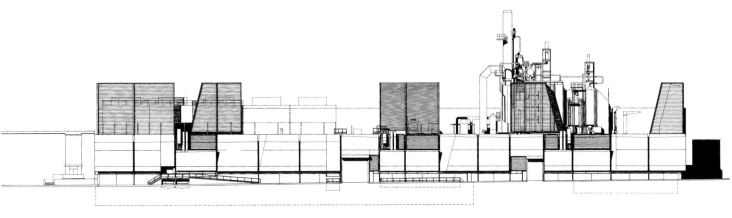

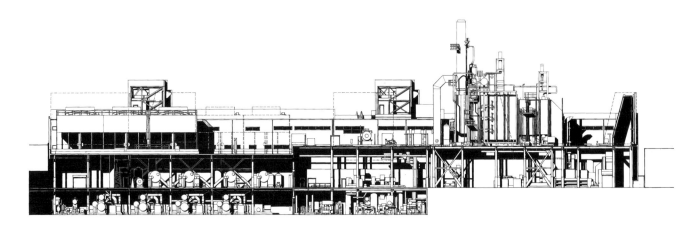

Pages 196/197
Holt Hinshaw Pfau Jones
UCLA Cogeneration Facility
Los Angeles, California, 1990–94
Wes Jones, born in 1958 in Santa
Monica, has rapidly become one
of the most influential forces in
the debate about a technological
approach to contemporary
architecture. By combining a brick-
veneer base with a voluntarily
technological upper level in
this power and cooling plant, he
has implicitly posed the question
of the reliability of industry in the
face of such inevitable natural
forces as the earthquakes to which
southern California is prone.

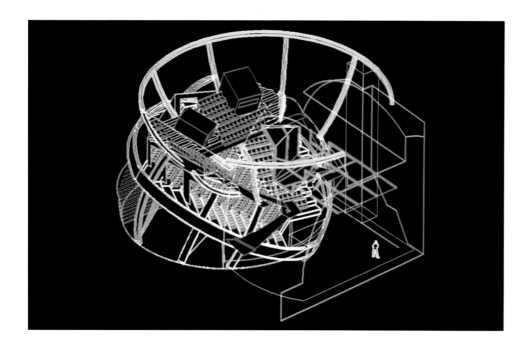

the work of Hermann Finsterlin. Deborah Dietsch brings these Johnson references up to date by writing about this pavilion, "It is inspired by the computer-generated forms of Frank O. Gehry and Peter Eisenman, German Expressionism, and the sculptural collages of Frank Stella. Clearly evident, too, is a link to the colorful dynamism of Zaha Hadid, whose drawings were shown in 'Deconstructivist Architecture,' which Johnson curated in 1988 at the Museum of Modern Art."[31] Changing styles frequently throughout his career, announcing the arrival of Post-Modernism for example with his AT&T Tower in New York, Philip Johnson has been more than a barometer of changes in fashion. As a mentor of architects like Michael Graves, or more recently Eric Owen Moss, he has exerted a clear and present influence on the course of American architecture. The building as an inhabited sculpture, a functional work of art, here reaches a viable presence that will be felt in architecture for a number of years to come.

Like a country onto itself, California has bred many internal solutions to the problems confronting contemporary architecture. Some of these can be seen through the work of younger architects like Wes Jones, Eric Owen Moss or Josh

Schweitzer. The University of California Los Angeles (UCLA) Energy Services Facility on the Brentwood campus is a container for gas turbines, boilers, chillers and exhaust stacks, plus miles of pipes, ducts and raceways. It represents an effort to come to grips with the impact, both visual and practical, of technology on architecture. As such it is far removed from the esthetic or geometric explorations of Philip Johnson's guest pavilion. The work of the San Francisco firm Holt Hinshaw Pfau Jones, and especially of Wes Jones, who has now formed Jones Partners-Architecture, this plant is intended to call into question the esthetic and intellectual place of technology in everyday life. In the earthquake zone of Los Angeles, it questions the supposed ability of technology to dominate nature. Solid, even massive, one might say that it has a curious San Francisco air to it. What is interesting about the investigation of Wes Jones is that he is exploring "the continuing possibilities of mechanically influenced architecture in the post-mechanical future." He has clearly thought about the implications of the new universe of electronics for architecture. As he says, "The dominance of the mechanical metaphor as a way of viewing the world is waning. In place of mechanical analogy and interpretation an explosion of electronic imagery – a mediated reality is asserting itself." But rather than trying to embrace the undefinable limits of "cyberspace" Jones declares, "The electronic will give the mechanical life, maybe even consciousness, while the mechanical will continue to give the electronic substance, will free it to have effect and act in the substantial world." Thus the consciously mechanical metaphor of the UCLA plant.[32]

The Kate Mantilini Restaurant by Morphosis on Wilshire Boulevard in Beverly Hills has already been mentioned above. It is an example of a different attitude toward technology that the critic Charles Jencks dubbed "Dead Tech, that is, High-Tech after the Bomb, or ecological catastrophe." As Jencks says, this "signified a

new, sophisticated attitude towards Modernism coming out of SCI-Arc, the avant-garde school of architecture that Thom Mayne's partner Michael Rotondi took over in the 1980s. Whereas Modernists had a faith in industrial progress, signified by the white sobriety of the International Style, the Post-Modernists of SCI-Arc had a bittersweet attitude toward technology. They knew it brought pollution, knew that progress in one place was paid for by regress in another, but nevertheless still loved industrial culture enough to remain committed to the Modernist impulse of dramatizing technology."[33]

Despite his cerebral approach, Morphosis principal Thom Mayne defines his work, such as the Kate Mantilini Restaurant, by making reference to film, albeit of the more intellectual variety: "Jim Jarmusch made the film *Stranger than Paradise* from nothing," he says. "Today, buildings are as ephemeral as film. The most solid aspect of my work is what has been published. The buildings are gone in ten years. Buildings are not that permanent anymore. There has got to be room in architecture for the Jim Jarmusches, not just the Spielbergs."[34]

Two projects by Eric Owen Moss, his Ince Theater, in Culver City, and Samitaur in the same Los Angeles area, illustrate this young architect's approach.

The Ince Theater is a 1994 project for a 450-seat theater to be located in the present parking lot between the Gary Group-Paramount Laundry-Lindblade Tower complex. Though not yet under construction, another part of this series of buildings, now called Metafor (formerly GEM), is being completed. Intended for live performance or movies, the Ince Theater's unusual form is a computer-generated interaction between three spheres. Whereas the other Gary Group buildings were largely conversions from existing warehouse space, the Ince Theater further explores the possibilities of spatial innovation that Moss proved himself to be capable of in the Lawson-Westen House (Brentwood, 1989–93). The apparent complexity of the structure as seen in computer drawings resolves itself into an unusual and elegant solution to the age-old problems of theater design. According to the original plans, a pedestrian bridge would link the theater to the as yet unbuilt Sony building across the street. The presence of Sony would make the idea of a theater in this otherwise rather forlorn section of Los Angeles more viable. Exterior and interior stairs would make it possible to climb onto the roof. This is a dynamic form, and as Eric Owen Moss has said, "If a building itself can include oppositions, so that it is about movement or the movement of ideas, then it might be more durable."

Pages 200/201
Eric Owen Moss
Samitaur
Culver City, California, 1990–96
It was in 1989 that the developer Frederick Norton Smith first spoke to Eric Owen Moss about the project that was to become Samitaur. Moss compares its most sculptural element, the "entry piece," (left), alternately to a cone, a cylinder, a pumpkin or an hour-glass. A planned second phase building, called "The Hook," would be granted a zoning variance to reach a total height of 38 m, adding even more credence to Moss's own appreciation of the project: "The area isn't sacrosanct, but still has residual meaning; the new changes the old, but doesn't blot it out."

Samitaur in Culver City challenges the use of urban space in a slightly different way than previous warehouse conversions imagined by Eric Owen Moss, because it is built over a road. Supported by steel columns that are positioned to avoid truck-loading docks and existing structures, the enigmatic shape of this building disguises a relatively straightforward internal plan. Samitaur is in fact a prototype for an ambitious project that Moss calls A.R. City (Air Rights City), which would be built in space above abandoned Southern Pacific Railroad Lines between Culver City and the difficult South-Central district of Los Angeles. Where other architects might dream only of working on pristine sites, Moss, working with the developer Frederick Norton Smith, has demonstrated that blighted semi-industrial urban areas can be profitably converted into viable office space. The cachet added by a talented architect makes such adaptive reuse and complementary construction, as in the case of Samitaur, all the more palatable to fashion-conscious clients. As John Morris Dixon has written, "Arguably, some of Moss's work could be considered" art, "in the sense that its formal intervention goes far beyond utilitarian purposes. On the other hand, his designs convert solid but underutilized industrial structures into places that serve very real purposes for the owners, the tenants, and the municipalities. Perhaps the Moss-Smith projects can set an example for the world beyond L.A."[35]

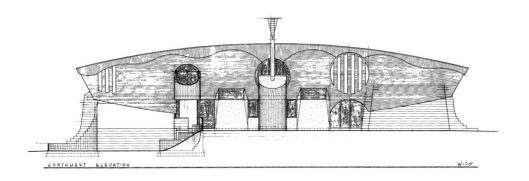

NORTHWEST ELEVATION

Pages 202/203
Bart Prince
Mead/Penhall Residence
Albuquerque, New Mexico,
1992–93
Built on a restricted 20 x 41 m
lot, this low construction cost
residence calls on the "organic
architecture" vocabulary of Prince
while making use of modern
materials such as galvanized
metal siding. Sculptural, and
almost anthropomorphic, the
Mead/Penhall residence is an
example of contemporary
American architecture that
is not part of the usual widely
published trends.

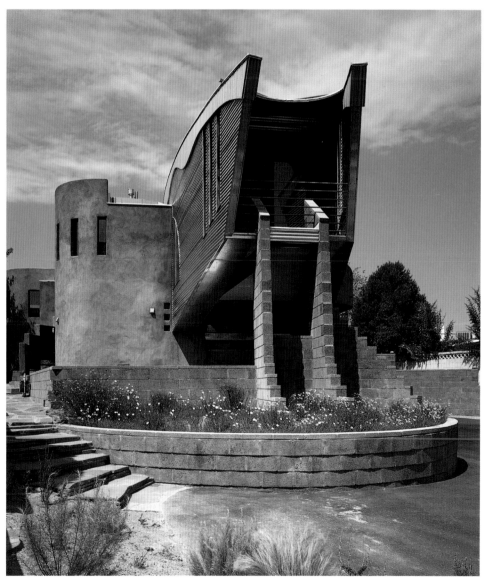

In a very different style, the sculptural appearance of Josh Schweitzer's Monument at Joshua Tree mentioned above is another reminder that California continues to play a role in a redefinition of the relationship between art and architecture. Indeed, the Southwestern United States, because of its largely favorable climate and because of the rapid growth of certain cities, has proven to be the area from which some of the most innovative new architecture has come in recent years.

Although a bit out of the architectural mainstream, Bart Prince, based in New Mexico, has created numerous private residences, some of which were clearly influenced by his mentor Bruce Goff. The Mead/Penhall Residence, in Albuquerque, New Mexico, however, represents an original solution to the economic problems so often posed to contemporary architects. Designed with a very low construction budget and simple materials such as exposed, sandblasted concrete block for walls around the carport, wood framing finished either with stucco and sheetrock or galvanized metal on the exterior and rough-sawn cedar plywood panels on the interior, this house sits on a lot that is only 20 x 41 m in size. Houses on nearby lots are one- and two-story contractor-designed frame/stucco structures, with a carport in front of each one. The design here was completed with the idea of providing space for a collection of photographs, paintings and nineteenth century furniture. There is a continuous curving ceiling made with exposed joists and metal. A series of covered and uncovered decks on the roof level emphasizes the distant mountain views to the north and east. It is particularly interesting to see Bart Prince's efficient and visually spectacular approach to a low-budget project.

An area that this volume has not delved into in detail is that of ecologically oriented or "green" architecture. Often setting aside esthetic reasoning to reduce energy consumption or to use non-polluting materials, green architecture is a significant and growing trend both in the United States and in Europe. One of the early proponents of an ecologically sensitive approach to architecture, James

Pages 204/205
SITE
Trawsfynydd Nuclear Power Station Decommissioning
North Wales, Great Britain, 1994
(project)

These two images show the current state of this nuclear power plant, built in 1959, which has recently ceased to function, and the way it would look should SITE's proposal be enacted. Asked to propose a new use for the site by a BBC-sponsored television producer, James Wines and SITE carefully studied the process of "phyto-remediation," which may permit the use of certain plants that absorb radioactivity to be used to accelerate the process of removal of the toxicity associated with the plant.

Wines, principal of the New York firm SITE (Sculpture in the Environment), was asked by a BBC-sponsored television producer in the fall of 1994, together with three other architects, to develop a proposal for the decommissioning of a nuclear power station in North Wales. Trawsfynydd (pronounced Traus-ven-ith) is the first major nuclear power plant in Great Britain to be decommissioned, but it is estimated that more than 400 plants worldwide will go out of service within the next twenty years. The owner of the plant, British Nuclear Electric, has developed a process called "Early Reduced Height Safestore," which according to the President of SITE, James Wines, amounts to simply closing down production and "leaving the dangerous radioactive core to be removed by the North Wales community in 2136 when it is considered safer to dismantle it." The proposal of SITE, obviously unpopular with British Nuclear Electric because of the high costs involved, would provide for a "rapid" decommissioning using robotics (remote operated vehicles to remove the core materials). They also suggest "a massive greening of the entire area, lake shore, and nuclear electric buildings using moss, rag weed and ivy as a means of removal of toxins from soil and water through the biochemical reaction of certain natural vegetation to radioactive materials." Finally, SITE proposes the construction on a nearby hillside of a communications center intended to explore the problems of decommissioning and alternative energy sources. Based on a "combination of a Celtic cross and the typical layered mounds of a Neolithic monument," this center, like many of SITE's projects, would be covered with greenery to an extent that it would "become increasingly metamorphic in its physical appearance and less and less visible within its natural context." Another group involved in this hypothetical design project, Arup Associates, suggested burying the plant in waste from nearby slate mines. On these mounds, Arups proposed to plant grass, moss and rings of trees. Because of the capacity of slate to absorb or insulate from radiation this solution does not seem inappropriate, and it too harkens back to the burial mounds of the earliest phases of Western civilization.

It is interesting to note that despite the very different location, and the fundamentally apocalyptic nature of the problem to be solved, architects have devised schemes for North Wales that in a way call on the very distant, in this case Neolithic past. Built by Sir Basil Spence in 1959, the Trawsfynydd complex was then viewed as an impressive monument to a new era of progress and plenty. It is ironic and significant that 35 years later this "Brave New World" becomes, on the contrary, a menacing symbol of the dangers of industrial growth. Herbert Muschamp, in *The New York Times,* put it this way: "Today, after decades of increasing public awareness of ecological issues, a visitor is more likely to see the twenty-story plant as a monstrous intruder in an Arcadian setting. Nuclear power, so the reasoning went, tapped into the innermost mysteries of nature. Why couldn't it coexist harmoniously with forests and lakes? Today, this kind of thinking is recognized as an integral part of cold war propaganda."[36] It would seem highly unlikely that British Nuclear Electric, or indeed other such similar companies elsewhere in the world, would call on qualified outside architects, let alone ecologically oriented groups such as SITE, for assistance in decommissioning. Most electrical companies prefer to give the impression that there really is no problem. As the London newspaper *The Independent* has written, however: "By 2010, more than 50,000 megawatts of current nuclear plant (the equivalent of 86 Trawsfynydds) will be made redundant in Britain. Each power station will cost something like £600 million to "decommission"

and about 135 years to lose its lethal potency."[37] It is difficult to judge whether the "phyto-remediation" proposed by SITE could really significantly alter the normal rate of absorption of radioactive elements. This is a matter more for scientists than for architects. It is certain, however, that blind faith in technological progress has led to extremely dangerous situations, and away from the earthbound wisdom of previous centuries.

Pages 206/207
SITE
Trawsfynydd Nuclear Power
Station Decommissioning
North Wales, Great Britain, 1994
(project)
Along with the actual decommissioning of the power plant itself, SITE proposed the construction of an International Energy Communications Center, whose ecologically sensitive form would be inspired by certain layered Neolithic burial mounds known in the region (right). Though probably not a practical solution to the problem posed by old nuclear power plants, this project does draw attention to the dilemma that they pose.

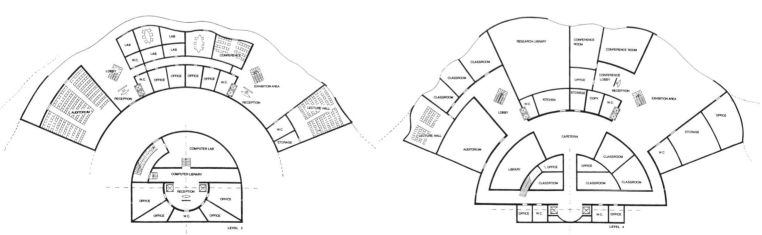

The European Crucible

Sir Norman Foster's 1995 project for the SECC Conference Center, in Glasgow, designed with the assistance of the engineers Ove Arup & Partners, is a stunning example of the type of new form being proposed by European architects. This is a £30 million 3,000 seat facility intended to complement the existing Scottish Exhibition and Conference Center. It is located on the banks of the river Clyde, on what was once Queen's Dock, which inspired its form "reminiscent of a series of ships' hulls." The hull or steel shell image seen here may bring to mind Jorn Utzon's Sydney Opera House, but there is a more regular and less overtly expressive rhythm in the Glasgow project. As the architect says, "The building's form is derived from the ideal relationship of the internal planning which wraps accommodation in a series of layers around the auditorium... The slots between the shells allow daylight to flood into the foyer spaces around the auditorium, they also allow views back towards Glasgow along the river Clyde." Presented in the kind of CAD view that architects and clients favor more and more frequently, Foster's Glasgow project is significant of current efforts to create forward-looking architecture that retains a deep connection to its site and local history.

Erick van Egeraat, former principal of the Dutch firm Mecanoo, recently completed the renovation of a building for the Nationale Nederlanden and ING Bank in Budapest, Hungary. Van Egeraat carefully restored this white 1882 Italianate building located on Andrassy ùt – the local equivalent of the Champs-Élysées. From street level, it seems that hardly anything has changed, but the two top floors added by the architect are dominated by the "whale," an organic blob that bursts through the glass roof onto the skyline of Budapest. Containing the boardroom, this extrusion is the focus of the project. It appears to float on a plane of glass, which also functions as the roof. Its organic forms contrast with the exposed lift machinery. All the more significant in Budapest because the city has undergone a period of fifty years in which architectural innovation was all but excluded, this unusual combination of late nineteenth and late twentieth century architecture is the fruit of the collaboration between the huge Internationale Nederlanden Groep NV (ING) represented by the Czech born Paul Koch now living in Holland and the architects. ING is the group that bought Barings Bank after its financial fiascoes in March 1995. It is one of Europe's largest banking and insurance companies, with a 1994 net profit of $1.49 billion. An admirer of Jean Nouvel, Frank O. Gehry and Van Egeraat, ING's representative Paul Koch has commissioned them to work in Prague. Gehry's much publicized Rasin building in Prague, called "Fred and Ginger" or the "Dancing Building" and attacked by Prince Charles, is the result of work carried out by ING, again represented by Koch, the Prague-based Sarajevo born architect Vladimir Milunic and Gehry himself. Like Gehry's Bilbao Museum, this design was made with the Dassault program CATIA, and another 3D computer modeling program called Pro/ENGINEER. Together with the CATIA models, Gehry "provided an AutoCAD 3D translation to local Czech architects for precasting operations and field erection," further proof of the advances made in computer technology in facilitating innovative design.[38] Clearly, in order for innovative architects to be given a chance to make the shape of the built environment evolve, it is necessary for them to have clients who are willing to take risks. This condition has unfortunately been met far too rarely at a time of rising economic and political conservatism. The Budapest Nationale Nederlanden and ING building deals with the problems of the renovation of an historic structure in an unusual way, and it is interesting to note that the American magazine *Architecture* wrote in its November 1995 editorial that "One has only to look at the glass mansard and cocoon designed by the Dutch architect... atop an Italianate block in Budapest to understand how experimental design energizes old buildings through contrast. It is difficult to imagine preservationists in this country sanctioning such juxtapositions."[39]

Page 209
Sir Norman Foster
SECC Conference Center
Glasgow, Scotland, 1995 (project)
This computer-generated image of a future facility to be located on the banks of the river Clyde demonstrates the increasing impact on architecture not only of CAD, but also of computer imagery as a method to explain to clients and to the public what an unbuilt structure will look like in its final form. This type of image may well encourage greater public interest in architecture in its planning phases.

Although less poetic than his Unazuki Meditation Space, the Takaoka Station in Japan, by the Barcelona architect Enric Miralles, contains very similar sculptural elements. Moving beyond the applied decoration that has been anathema to modern architecture since the early part of the century, this project seeks to integrate an exuberant manipulation of steel forms with the entrance to a railroad station. Indeed, the point made by Miralles and others about the new-found freedom of architecture to explore the range of possibilities offered by the world of art is not that architecture should embody the notion of "art for art's sake." Rather what is sought here is a renewal of the vocabulary of the built environment, an enrichment that can only seek out ways to make the experience of entering and using a building more enlightening and fulfilling. After the long period in which functionality ruled above any other consideration, this search for new forms must be hailed as a true liberation of architecture.

Christian de Portzamparc's Palais des Congrès project in Paris, already mentioned above, brings to the fore the problems posed by the reuse or expansion of modern buildings. Whereas, prior to the twentieth century, large urban structures were often designed as though they were to last forever, economic considerations and evolving attitudes toward architecture imposed the construction of an enormous number of buildings that clearly were not meant to withstand the force of time. Less sensitive esthetically than the question of older buildings whose facades are

Pages 210/211
Erick van Egeraat
Nationale Nederlanden
and ING Bank
Budapest, Hungary, 1993–95

Erick van Egeraat added two stories and an organic "whale" shape to the top of an 1882 Italianate building on the Andrassy ùt in Budapest, no small feat in a city used to the stultification of the communist regimes of the post-war period. This interesting combination of organic and mechanical elements signals a departure both from the "deconstructivist" trends of the late 1980s and from the even more recent minimalism of the neo-modern movement.

now often carefully restored in Western countries, that of modern buildings that have outlived their initial usefulness will increasingly be posed to architects.

Portzamparc's Bandai Tower, an entirely new building to be located in Tokyo, is an unusual effort to use a system of variable colored lighting to "sculpt" the facade at night. This is a 7,000 m² complex including offices for the toy company, apartments, a restaurant and flexible events spaces. As Jean-Pierre Le Dantec, author of a recent monograph on Portzamparc has written about the Bandai project, "This is art. It is an art of light and space as it is conceived of by such demanding creators as Robert Irwin, James Turrell or Robert Wilson."[40]

Officially inaugurated on June 29, 1995, the European Court of Human Rights in Strasbourg, France, by English architect Sir Richard Rogers, is an outgrowth of the European Convention on Human Rights, signed in Rome on November 4, 1950, and applied since 1953. Through two branches, the Commission and the Court of Human Rights, this organization is in principle at the disposition of those persons who feel that their guaranteed human rights have been violated. Based in a 3,800 m² building in Strasbourg since 1962, the Court was granted a 2 ha plot of land, and asked to build a new 20,000 m² building by a resolution of the European Council of Ministers on April 26, 1986. The initially planned date for the inauguration, May 5, 1989, was not maintained, partially because the proposed architectural plans were found lacking. The city of Strasbourg, which granted the land, then organized a competition, and Sir Richard Rogers was chosen on September 19, 1989. Rogers

Enric Miralles
Takaoka Station
Takaoka, Japan, 1993–95
Calling on a sculptural, tubular form that brings to mind his Unazuki Meditation Center, Miralles innovates here in the area of the architectural significance of the canopy or signage that often signals the presence of a public building such as a railroad station. This is particularly unusual in Japan, where railroad station architecture is by and large unexceptional, despite the design of Hiroshi Hara's extraordinary Kyoto JR Station.

Sir Richard Rogers
European Court of Human Rights
Strasbourg, France, 1989–95
Calling on a high-tech vocabulary
that recalls the fact that he was
the co-author of the Centre
Georges Pompidou in Paris with
Renzo Piano in 1977, Rogers
engages in an attempt to symbolize function in an organization
headquarters that was initially
bipartite. Since that is no longer
the case, his symbolism will be
somewhat enigmatic for future
users, but such is the nature of
clients with which contemporary
architects are obliged to deal.

proposed a curved, double-headed building, corresponding to the bipartite function of the organization. When Rogers was chosen, the 240 million French franc construction cost corresponded to facilities for 25 member states, but with the fall of the Berlin Wall, that number increased to 34, and 3,000 m^2 of new office space were added to the project in the spring of 1992. The final cost increased to 455 million French francs by December 1994. The final project, a 28,000 m^2 structure, includes 860 m^2 for the main court room, 520 m^2 for the meeting room of the Commission, 4,500 m^2 of meeting rooms, and 16,500 m^2 for the offices.

It should be noted that the so-called "Protocol 11" signed by all of the member states since May 11, 1994, and already ratified by nine of them, provides that the current bipartite organization will be dissolved in favor of a unique court structure. Through no fault of his own, the very symbolism of Sir Richard Rogers's building thus no longer corresponds to the actual function of the European Court of Human Rights.

Born in 1933 in Florence, a former partner of Sir Norman Foster and Renzo Piano, with whom he built the Centre Pompidou, Rogers is seen as a leading proponent of the so-called "High Tech" style in architecture, an image reinforced by buildings such as his London headquarters for the Lloyd's insurance groups. Rogers has clearly thought about the future of architecture, as the prescient remarks he made in February 1995 certainly show:

"The art of building is pursued almost exclusively for single-minded commercial

Sir Richard Rogers
European Court of Human Rights
Strasbourg, France, 1989–95
With its sweeping office wings
following the curve of the Ill River,
the European Court of Human
Rights provides a suitably contemporary image for an organization
whose membership has expanded
greatly along with the recent
political modifications in Europe.
Indeed this fact means that the
original design, conceived for
a smaller Europe, had to be
enlarged, and may soon prove
to be of insufficient size.

Pages 216/217
Aldo Rossi
Hotel Il Palazzo
Fukuoka, Japan, 1988–89
The result of a fruitful collaboration between this Milanese
architect and designers such as
the late Shiro Kuramata, the
Palazzo Hotel is an island of calm
and comparative luxury in the
bustling, chaotic environment of
the commercial center of Fukuoka.
Its blank facade may have more
to do with Roman tombs than with
Japanese temples, but curiously
in an architectural environment
where anything goes, this block of
marble and copper does not seem
as incongruous as it might.

objectives. Our 'bottom line' economies ensure that there is no incentive to invest in ecological technologies that only pay off in the long run.

After a century of refinement, the steel or concrete building has never been so cheap to build, nor built so cheaply.

While buildings of all types are being packaged and standardized, architects are being selected on the basis of lowest fees rather than the quality of their work. Designing greater flexibility into our modern buildings inevitably moves architecture away from fixed and perfect forms. But when a society needs buildings that are capable of responding to changing requirements, I believe we must search for new forms that express the power of change.

Restoring old buildings to their supposed original condition is, I would argue, a spurious notion. Buildings have always been adapted, reshaped, redecorated, replumbed and relit. But this living process grinds to a halt in the face of over-zealous preservation. Today, we are letting our architectural heritage choke our future. Making museums of our cities ossifies society.

Rather than rely on high-energy consumption, architects are now beginning to explore building forms and technologies that harness natural resources — landscape, wind, sun, earth and water.

Computer technology is one of the breakthroughs in the design of low-energy buildings. Programs now available can generate models that predict air movement, light levels and heat gain while the buildings are still on the drawing board. This significantly increases our ability to refine each aspect of the design of a building, so as to maximize the use of its natural environment. And it is computers that are giving buildings increasingly sensitive electronic nervous systems, able to register internal and external conditions and respond to individual needs. New materials

exist that are capable of changing from high insulation to low, from opaque to transparent, that can react organically to the environment, respond to the daily environmental cycle and transform themselves through the seasons. The future is here, but its impact on architecture is only just beginning."[41]

The Milanese architect Aldo Rossi, born in 1931, and known for his rather radical political views and for a certain Post-Modern taste, built two notable structures in recent years. His Maastricht Museum is a large exhibition hall located in a former factory area on the banks of the Maas River. Its central, metallic element has been compared in form by critics to a coffee pot, but the essential inspiration of this structure comes from the early twentieth century industrial architecture of the area, which has been for the most part razed. His Palazzo Hotel, located in Fukuoka,

Japan, is a different matter. Here, amidst the typical visual chaos of the Japanese urban environment, in the Haruyoshi area, he has erected a seven-story hotel whose facade, covered in marble and copper, contains no apparent windows. This unexpected, almost funerary design gives the structure a kind of calm, imposing presence. Initially intended as the starting point for the renewal of a larger area, the Palazzo Hotel is a fascinating attempt at collaborative design. Within Rossi's architecture, Gaetano Pesce, Ettore Sottsass, Shiro Kuramata and Alfredo Arribas have designed bars and discothèques. Unfortunately the promoter Matsuhiro Kuzuwa, who had the vision to call on this exceptional group of creators, was not able to pursue his larger plans, but the Palazzo remains a witness to the openness of some Japanese clients and the inventiveness of European architecture and design.

Whereas Rossi's Palazzo bears the evident signs of ample construction and

design budgets, Schneider + Schumacher's Info Box in Berlin is almost a diametrical opposite. A temporary exhibition building designed to inform residents about the massive construction projects under way in Berlin, the Info Box would appear to be a prototypical architecture for the age of uncertainty. It is only in recent years that talented architects have turned their attention in any serious way to the problems posed by ephemeral structures. This may be due to a lack of demand, or to the egos of some architects who still try to build "for eternity." Naturally there have been consistent efforts throughout the twentieth century to grapple with the concept of non-permanent architecture, through inflatable buildings or the geodesic domes of Buckminster Fuller for example. Universal exhibitions have been a constant source of ideas for ephemeral architecture, to the extent that some "temporary" structures such as the Tour Eiffel in Paris have become much more

permanent than their designers intended. As cities expand and tight budgets preclude the construction of durable architecture in some locations, as the problems of homeless people become unbearable, it would appear that buildings such as the Info Box might very soon be called upon to do more than house exhibitions. It would be all the better if architects took the time to resolve the esthetic and practical problems of temporary structures in a way that might make them more livable than if they are conceived in a more mechanical or purely industrial way.

The talented Portuguese architect Alvaro Siza, winner of the 1992 Pritzker Prize, was called on in 1991 to design a manufacturing hall for the Vitra complex in Weil am Rhein, Germany, already mentioned in this volume because of the projects built there by Frank O. Gehry, Zaha Hadid and Tadao Ando. Located next to Hadid's fire station and across the road from buildings by Nicholas Grimshaw and Frank O. Gehry, this factory facility faced unusual challenges of context. Indeed, there are very few places in the world where such a concentration of buildings built by "name" architects exists. Siza's solution was to erect a reinforced concrete structure with a nearly blank red brick wall facing the street. At 11,600 m² this is the largest structure on the Vitra "campus," although its very blankness calls attention less to its bulk than to the neighboring, more exuberant forms of Hadid. An 11 m high steel bridge arches across the road toward Grimshaw's factory building, and frames the view toward the fire station for entering visitors. Such fundamental modesty is undoubtedly rare amongst the architects cited in this volume, who do, it is true, have a natural tendency to call attention to themselves.

One excellent European example of ecologically sensitive architecture must be cited here. The new Ulm University Engineering Sciences (Universität Ulm Elektrotechnik/Hochfrequenztechnik, 1990–91) buildings are located in a peripheral, almost rural setting. The architect Otto Steidle says that he "mistrusts all buildings which only have one possible function," and in Ulm his efforts have been directed toward not creating "a world for specialists, but more an indicator of the

Pages 220/221
Otto Steidle
Ulm University
Ulm, Germany, 1990–91
Located between the city of Ulm and the Oberer Eselsberg, this brightly colored university complex calls on principles of ecology and economical construction. Close to Richard Meier's rather substantial Daimler-Benz Research Center, Steidle's lighthearted particle board and concrete barriers do not seem to be on quite the same wavelength, but it may well be that the European's point of view is more in keeping with the spirit of the 1990s than is the American's weighty monumentality.

links between and the closeness of art and science." This theoretical input is of course interesting, but the final result is more than a little surprising, with its heavy reliance on inexpensive materials such as plywood (for budgetary reasons again), and its complex, colorful facades. The color scheme is visually based on a rhythmic diagram of Bach's Fugue in C minor, which does not prevent the whole from having a slightly prison-like appearance, perhaps due to the towers erected at the nodal points of the complex. Seeking, as he was asked to do by local officials, not to upset the Obere Eselsberg site in its function as an important climatic factor for Ulm, Otto Steidle has created numerous passageways between the forest side and the opposite direction, corresponding to Richard Meier's nearby Research Center for Daimler-Benz. The whole university complex is built with an environmental respect symbolized by a rainwater-gathering and distribution system. Together with the substantial use of wood in the upper sections, these design elements undoubtedly qualify the Ulm University as an ecologically sound structure. Perhaps more fundamentally significant in architectural terms, the flexibility of the design, or in some sense its intellectual modesty in the positive sense of the term, signals a very different approach than that which might have been taken a few years ago, when strict Modernism, or worse, Post-Modernism were in vogue.

A final project, the L'Oréal Factory at Aulnay-sous-Bois, France, by the architects Valode & Pistre, is in many ways symbolic of the search for new forms in architecture. This 30,000 m² manufacturing and administrative complex is most notably marked by its enormous curved roof inspired by the image of a three-petaled flower floating above the ground. Made of an aluminum/polyethylene "sandwich," the

Pages 222/223
Valode & Pistre
L'Oréal Factory
Aulnay-sous-Bois, France,
1988–91
Although the initial design was
inspired by the form of a three-
petaled orchid (Phalenopsis), the
resulting shape, visible in one
of the original drawings by Denis
Valode (left), took on a futuristic
allure, which enabled the
architects to provide bright,
column-free workspace around
the central garden.

roof elements, measuring 60 x 130 m are suspended without columns by a tubular spaceframe superstructure designed by the late engineer Peter Rice. The apparent and real lightness of the roof structure made it possible to bring far more light into the factory areas than is usually the case. Because of new production techniques, dividing the usual assembly line process of this cosmetics manufacturer into smaller units, the architects were able to propose this spectacular tripartite structure disposed around a central garden and artificial lake, rather than adhering to the more traditional rectilinear architecture of factories. The unusual curving complexity of the roof elements was made possible not only by computer-aided design but by a laser-guided checking system for the placement of the 20,000 panels. Combining an innovative structural solution with a renewed concept of factory layout, this project concludes this survey as well as any other. The L'Oréal factory shows that technology, new materials and a willingness on the part of clients and architects to experiment have created the conditions for a true renewal of architecture. In their project description, Valode & Pistre quote Alvar Aalto, who said, "Architecture has an unstated ideal, which is to recreate paradise. If we did not constantly bear this idea in mind, all of our buildings would be simpler and more trivial, and life would become . . . yes, it would almost no longer be worth living."

Pages 224/225
Valode & Pistre
L'Oréal Factory
Aulnay-sous-Bois, France,
1988–91
This factory for a cosmetics manufacturer located on the outskirts of Paris is a technical *tour de force*. The 7,023 aluminum and polyethylene composite panels that make up the roof are each attached at four points, three of which are adjustable in all three dimensions. Their installation required no less than 21,000 adjustments made on site.

Notes

1 Wigley, Mark, in: *Deconstructivist Architecture*, The Museum of Modern Art, New York 1988.

2 Ibid.

3 Gehry, Frank O., in: *The Pritzker Architecture Prize, 1989, Frank Owen Gehry*, The Hyatt Foundation, Chicago 1990.

4 Ghiradro, Diane: Eisenman's Bogus Avant-Garde, *Progressive Architecture,* November 1994.

5 Eisenman, Peter, interview, 40 West 25th Street, New York, May 15, 1995.

6 Pearce, Martin: From Urb to Bit, in: *Architects in Cyberspace,* Architectural Design, London 1995.

7 Tschumi, Bernard, in: *Deconstructivist Architecture,* The Museum of Modern Art, New York 1988.

8 Mayne, Thom, interview, Morphosis Architects, 2041 Colorado Avenue, Santa Monica, May 12, 1994.

9 Moss, Eric Owen, interview, 8557 Higuera Street, Culver City, May 14, 1994.

10 Eisenman, Peter, interview, 40 West 25th Street, New York, May 15, 1995.

11 Solomon, Nancy: Computer-aided manufacturing, in: *Architecture,* November 1995.

12 Goldberger, Paul: *The Skyscraper*, Alfred A. Knopf, New York 1981.

13 Hara, Hiroshi: *GA Architect 13*, A.D.A. Edita, Tokyo 1993.

14 Eisenman, Peter, in: *Architecture Beyond Architecture, Creativity and Social Transformations in Islamic Cultures*, Edited by Cynthia Davidson, Academy Editions, London 1995.

15 Holl, Steven, in: *The End of Architecture?*, Edited by Peter Noever, Prestel, Munich 1993.

16 *Art and Power*, The Hayward Gallery, London 1995.

17 Fuksas, Massimiliano, interview, M.F. France, 76 bis rue Vieille du Temple, Paris, October 12, 1995.

18 Kabakov, Ilya: *Installations 1983–1995*, Centre Georges Pompidou, Paris 1995.

19 Enric Miralles, in: *El Croquis,* 72(II), Madrid 1995.

20 Perrault, Dominique, interview, February 3, 1995.

21 Riley, Terry, in: *Light Construction*, The Museum of Modern Art, New York 1995.

22 *The Independent,* October 26, 1994.

23 Lin, Maya, interview, May 25, 1995.

24 Meier, Richard, interview, Richard Meier & Partners, Los Angeles, May 16, 1994.

25 Frazer, John: The Architectural Relevance of Cyberspace, in: *Architects in Cyberspace,* Architectural Design, London 1995.

26 *Itsuko Hasegawa,* Architectural Monographs, n° 31, Academy Editions, London 1993.

27 *Toyo Ito*, JA Library 2, Summer 1993, Shinkenchiku-sha Co., Ltd., Tokyo.

28 *Fumihiko Maki*, The Japan Architect, n° 16, Winter 1994, Shinkenchiku-sha Co., Ltd., Tokyo.

29 Eisenman, Peter, interview, 40 West 25th Street, New York, May 15, 1995.

30 Muschamp, Herbert: A monster of a masterpiece in Connecticut, in: *The New York Times,* September 17, 1995.

31 Dietsch, Deborah: Philip's Folly, *Architecture,* November 1995.

32 Jones, Wes: *The mech in tecture, Any,* n° 10, January 1995.

33 Jencks, Charles: *Heteropolis, Los Angeles, The Riots and the Strange Beauty of Hetero-Architecture*, 1993.

34 Mayne, Thom, interview, Santa Monica, May 12, 1994.

35 Dixon, John Morris: Superstructure, *Progressive Architecture,* July 1995.

36 Muschamp, Herbert: Building on the ruins of temples to nuclear power, *The New York Times,* April 2, 1995.

37 Glancey, Jonathan: Ideas beyond the nuclear station, *The Independent,* April 12, 1995.

38 Computer-controlled curvature. Rasin Office Building, Prague, Czech Republic, Frank O. Gehry & Associates, *Architecture,* November 1995.

39 Dietsch, Deborah: Preservation needs better architecture, Editorial, *Architecture,* November 1995.

40 Le Dantec, Jean-Pierre: *Christian de Portzamparc*, Editions du Regard, Paris 1995.

41 Rogers, Richard: The imperfect form of the new, The Reith Lectures, *The Independent,* February 27, 1995.

BIOGRAPHIES

Tadao Ando

Born in Osaka in 1941, Tadao Ando was self-educated as an architect, largely through his travels in the United States, Europe and Africa (1962–69). He founded Tadao Ando Architect & Associates in Osaka in 1969. He has received the Alvar Aalto Medal, Finnish Association of Architects (1985); Medaille d'or, French Academy of Architecture (1989); the 1992 Carlsberg Prize; and the 1995 Pritzker Prize. He has taught at Yale (1987), Columbia (1988), and Harvard (1990). Notable buildings include: Rokko Housing, Kobe (1983–93); Church on the Water, Hokkaido (1988); Japan Pavilion Expo '92, Seville, Spain (1992); Forest of Tombs Museum, Kumamoto (1992); and the Suntory Museum, Osaka (1994). Current projects include new housing for Kobe, and a large complex on the island of Awaji.

Arquitectonica

Bernardo Fort-Brescia was born in Lima, Peru in 1951. B. Arch., Princeton, 1973. M. Arch., Harvard, 1975. Principal of Arquitectonica since founding in 1977 in Miami. Laurinda Hope Spear was born in Rochester, MN, in 1950. M. Arch. Columbia, 1975. Master in City Planning, M.I.T. Principal of Arquitectonica with her husband since its founding. Major projects: Spear House, Miami (1976–78); The Palace, Miami (1979–82); The Atlantis, Miami (1980–82); Mulder House, Lima, Peru (1983–85); Banco de Crédito, Lima, Peru (1983–88); North Dade Justice Center, Miami (1984–87); Center for Innovative Technology, Herndon, VA (1985–88); and Banque de Luxembourg Headquarters, Luxembourg, 1994.

Mario Botta

Born in 1943 in Mendrisio, Switzerland, Mario Botta left school at the age of fifteen to become an apprentice in a Lugano architectural office. He designed his first house the following year. After completing his studies in Milan and Venice, Botta worked briefly in the entourage of Le Corbusier, Louis Kahn and Luigi Snozzi. He built numerous private houses in Cadenazzo (1970–71), Riva San Vitale (1971–73), and Ligornetto (1975–76). The Médiathèque in Villeurbanne (1984–88) and the Cultural Center in Chambèry (1982–87) followed. Current projects include the Évry Cathedral (1988–1995), the Tamaro Chapel with the artist Enzo Cucchi in Switzerland, a church in Mogno, and a telecommunications center in Bellinzona.

Architecture Studio

Created in 1973, Architecture Studio has six principals: Rodo Tisnado, Martin Robain, Alain Bretagnolle, René-Henri Arnaud, Jean-François Bonne and Laurent-Marc Fischer. Their first major building was the Institut du Monde Arabe (1981–87), designed with Nouvel, Soria and Lézénès. Other significant buildings include the Embassy of France in Muscat, Oman (1987–89); and the Lycée du Futur, Jaunay-Clan, France (1986–87); and the University Restaurant, Dunkerque, France (1991–93). Current work includes the Institut national du Judo, Paris, France (1988–96); and above all, the European Parliament in Strasbourg, France (1994–97).

Asymptote

Lise Ann Couture was born in Montreal in 1959. She received her B. Arch. from Carlton University, Canada, and M. Arch. from Yale. She is presently a Design Critic in the Master of Architecture program at Parsons School of Design, New York. Hani Rashid received his M. Arch. degree from the Cranbrook Academy of Art, Bloomfield Hills, MI. He is currently Adjunct Assistant Professor at the Columbia University Graduate School of Architecture, New York. They created Asymptote in 1987. Projects include their 1989 fourth place entry for the Alexandria Library, a commissioned housing project for Brig, Switzerland, and their participation in the 1993 competition for an art center in Tours, France (1993).

Will Bruder

Born in Milwaukee, Wisconsin, in 1946, Will Bruder has a B.A. degree in sculpture from the University of Wisconsin-Milwaukee, and is self-trained as an architect. He apprenticed under Paolo Soleri and Gunnar Birkerts. He obtained his architecture licence in 1974 and created his own studio the same year. He studied at the American Academy in Rome for six months in 1987. He has taught and lectured at SCI-Arc, Yale, Taliesin West and Georgia Tech. Current projects include Teton County Library, Jackson, WY; Riddell Advertising, Jackson, WY; Temple Kol Ami, Scottsdale, AZ; Deer Vallery Rock Art Center, Phoenix, AZ; and residences in Boston, Colorado, Arizona, Canada and Australia, as well as a restaurant in Manhattan.

Santiago Calatrava

Born in Valencia in 1951, Santiago Calatrava studied art and architecture at the Escuela Técnica Superior de Arquitectura in Valencia (1969–74) and engineering at the ETH in Zurich (doctorate in Technical Science, 1981). He opened his own architecture and civil engineering office the same year. His built work includes Gallery and Heritage Square, BCE Place, Toronto (1987–92); the Bach de Roda Bridge, Barcelona (1985–87); the Torre de Montjuic, Barcelona (1989–92); the Kuwait Pavilion at Expo '92, Seville; and the Alamillo Bridge for the same exhibition. He was a finalist in the competition for the Reichstag in Berlin, and plans to build a museum of science and a communications tower in Valencia.

Peter Eisenmann

Born in New York in 1932, B. Arch. Cornell, M. Arch. Columbia, Masters and Ph.D. degrees, University of Cambridge, Great Britain. Peter Eisenman has taught at Cambridge, Princeton, Yale and Harvard as well as the University of Illinois and Ohio State University. Main buildings: Wexner Center for the Visual Arts, Ohio State University, Columbus, OH (1982–89); Koizumi Sangyo Building, Tokyo, Japan (1987–89); Greater Columbus Convention Center, Columbus, OH (1989–93). Current projects include the Center for the Arts, Emory University, Atlanta, GA, and the Arnoff Center for Design and Art, University of Cincinnati, OH.

Massimiliano Fuksas

Born in Rome in 1944, Massimiliano Fuksas received his degree from the Faculty of Architecture in Rome in 1969. Created the architectural office "Granma" with Anna Maria Sacconi (1969–88). Having completed a large number of projects in Italy, he began to be known in both Italy and France as of the late 1980s with projects such as his new cemetery in Orvieto (1990), the town hall and library of Cassino (1990), and in France, the Médiathèque, Rézé (1991) and the École nationale d'Ingénieurs de Brest (ENIB, 1992). More recently, he completed the restructuring of a city block on the Rue Candie in Paris (1987–93). Current work includes the Lycée Technique in Alfortville, the Place des Nations in Geneva, a 150 m high tower in Vienna, and a large shopping center in Salzburg.

Nicholas Grimshaw

A 1965 graduate of the Architectural Association, Nicholas Grimshaw was born in 1939 in London. He created his present firm, Nicholas Grimshaw and Partners Ltd., in 1980. His numerous factory structures include those built for Herman Miller in Bath (1976), B.M.W. at Bracknell (1980), the furniture maker Vitra at Weil am Rhein, Germany (1981), and for the *Financial Times* in London in 1988. He also built houses associated with the Sainsbury Supermarket Development in Camden Town (1989), and the British Pavilion at the 1992 Universal Exhibition in Seville.

Erick van Egeraat

Born in 1956 in Amsterdam, Erick van Egeraat attended the Technical University Delft, Department of Architecture, from which he graduated in 1984. Professional practice since 1981. Co-founder of Mecanoo architects in Delft (1983). Founder of Erick van Egeraat Associated Architects (1995). Recent and current work includes: faculty building of the Faculties of Physics and Astronomy, University of Leiden (1988–96); Nature and Science Museum, Rotterdam (1989–95); Pop Art Exhibition, Kunsthal, Rotterdam, 1995; Housing Sternstrasse, Dresden (1994–); Leonardo da Vinci exhibition design, Rotterdam 1995–96, Kunsthal Rotterdam; reconstruction of the "Grote Markt" square east, Groningen; Utrecht Centrum Project, masterplan 1995–96.

Sir Norman Foster

Born in Manchester in 1935, Norman Foster studied at the University of Manchester and at Yale in 1963. After working briefly with Buckminster Fuller, he founded "Team 4" with Sir Richard Rogers, and created Foster Associates in 1967. Knighted in 1990, Sir Norman Foster has notably built the Sainsbury Center at the University of East Anglia, Norwich (1978); the Renault Distribution Center, Swindon (1983); the Hong Kong and Shanghai Bank tower in Hong Kong (1986); and the terminal for Stansted Airport (1981–91). Current projects include: the Commerzbank in Frankfurt, the tallest building in Europe; Hong Kong's new airport; and King's Cross Station in London.

Frank O. Gehry

Born in Toronto, Canada, in 1929, Frank O. Gehry studied at the University of Southern California, Los Angeles (1949–51), and at Harvard (1956–57). Principal of Frank O. Gehry and Associates, Inc., Los Angeles, since 1962, he received the 1989 Pritzker Prize. Some of his notable projects are the Loyola Law School, Los Angeles (1981–84); the Norton Residence, Venice, CA (1982–84); California Aerospace Museum, Los Angeles (1982–84); Schnabel Residence, Brentwood (1986–89); Festival Disney, Marne-la-Vallée, France (1988–92); University of Toledo Art Building, Toledo, OH (1990–92); American Center, Paris, France (1988–93); Disney Concert Hall, Los Angeles (construction temporarily halted); and the Guggenheim Museum, Bilbao, Spain (under construction).

Hiroshi Hara

Born in Kawasaki, Japan in 1936, Hiroshi Hara received his BA from the University of Tokyo (1959), his M.A. in 1961 and his Ph.D. from the same institution in 1964, before being an associate professor at the University's Faculty of Architecture. Though his first work dates from the early 1960s, he began his collaboration with Atelier φ in 1970. Notable structures include numerous private houses, such as his own residence, Hara House, Machida, Tokyo (1973–74). He participated in the 1982 International Competition for the Parc de la Villette, Paris; built the Yamato International Building (Ota-ku, Tokyo) 1985–86; the Iida City Museum, Iida, Nagano (1986–88); and the Sotetsu Culture Center, Yokohama, Kanagawa (1988–90). Recent work includes the Umeda Sky City, Kita-ku, Osaka (1988–93); and the Kyoto JR Station, Sakyo-ku, Kyoto (1990–97).

Itsuko Hasegawa

Itsuko Hasegawa was born in Shizuoka Prefecture in 1941. She graduated from Kanto Gakuin University in Yokohama in 1964. After working in the atelier of Kiyonori Kikutake (1964–69), she was a research student in the Department of Architecture of the Tokyo Institute of Technology. She was subsequently an assistant of Kazuo Shinohara in the same school (1971–78) before creating Itsuko Hasegawa Atelier (1979) in Tokyo. Her built work includes houses in Nerima (1986), Kumamoto (1986), and Higashitamagawa (1987). In more recent years, she has built on a larger scale: Shonandai Cultural Center, Fujisawa, Kanagawa (1987–90); Oshima-machi Picture Book Museum, Imizu, Toyama (1991–94); and the Sumida Culture Factory, Sumida, Tokyo (1991–94). She was the runner up in the 1993 competition for the new Cardiff Bay Opera House. She has lectured at Waseda University, at the Tokyo Institute of Technology, and in 1992 at the Harvard Graduate School of Design.

Hodgetts + Fung

The principals of Hodgetts + Fung, created in 1984, are Craig Hodgetts (B.A. Oberlin College, M. Arch., Yale) and Hsin-Ming Fung (M. Arch., UCLA). Aside from the Towell Temporary Library at UCLA, their work includes the Click & Flick Agency in Hollywood; a permanent solar exhibition environment at EMR's Bad Oeynhausen facility, L.A. Arts Park in the Sepulveda Basin, Hemdale Film Corporation Office facility, L.A.; and the Viso Residence (Hollywood). They designed the exhibition "Blueprints for Modern Living" at the MoCA Temporary Contemporary, and are currently working on a traveling exhibition of the work of Charles and Ray Eames, scheduled to open in Washington in 1997.

Arata Isozaki

Born in Oita City on the Island of Kyushu in 1931, Arata Isozaki graduated from the Architectural Faculty of the University of Tokyo in 1954 and established Arata Isozaki & Associates in 1963, having worked in the office Kenzo Tange. Winner of the 1986 Royal Institute of British Architects Gold Medal, he has been a juror of major competitions such as that held in 1988 for the new Kansai International Airport. Notable buildings include: the Museum of Modern Art, Gunma (1971–74); the Tsukuba Center Building, Tsukuba (1978–83); the Museum of Contemporary Art, Los Angeles (1981–86); Art Tower Mito, Mito (1986–90); Team Disney Building, Florida (1990–94); and B-con Plaza, Oita (1991–95). Current projects include Higashi Shizuoka Plaza Cultural Complex, Shizuoka; and Ohio's Center of Science and Industry (COSI), Columbus, Ohio.

Toyo Ito

Born in 1941 in Seoul, Korea, Toyo Ito graduated from the University of Tokyo in 1965, and worked in the office of Kiyonori Kikutake until 1969. He created his own office in 1971, assuming the name of Toyo Ito Architect & Associates in 1979. His completed work includes: the Silver Hut residence, Tokyo (1984); Tower of the Winds, Yokohama, Kanagawa (1986); Yatsushiro Municipal Museum Yatsushiro, Kumamoto (1989–91); and the Elderly People's Home (1992–94) and Fire Station (1992–95), both located in the same city on the island of Kyushu. He participated in the Shanghai Luijiazui Center Area International Planning and Urban Design Consultation in 1992, and has built a Public Kindergarten Frankfurt-Eckenheim, Germany (1988–91).

Herzog & de Meuron

Jacques Herzog and Pierre de Meuron were both born in Basel in 1950. They received degrees in architecture at the ETH in Zurich in 1975, after studying with Aldo Rossi, and founded their firm Herzog & de Meuron Architecture Studio in Basel in 1978. Their built work includes the Antipodes I Student Housing at the Université de Bourgogne, Dijon (1991–92); the Ricola Europe Factory and Storage Building in Mulhouse (1993); and a gallery for a private collection of contemporary art in Munich (1991–92). Most notably they were chosen early in 1995 to design the new Tate Gallery extension for contemporary art, to be situated in the Bankside Power Station, on the Thames, opposite St Paul's Cathedral.

Steven Holl

Born in 1947 in Bremerton, Washington. B. Arch., University of Washington, 1970, in Rome and at the Architectural Association in London (1976). Began his career in California and opened his own office in New York in 1976. Has taught at the University of Washington, Syracuse University, and, since 1981, at Columbia University. Notable buildings: Hybrid Building, Seaside, FL (1984–88); Berlin AGB Library, Berlin, Germany, competition entry (1988); Void Space/Hinged Space, Housing, Nexus World, Fukuoka, Japan (1989–91); Stretto House, Dallas, TX (1989–92); Makuhari Housing, Chiba, Japan (1992–97); and Museum of Contemporary Art, Helsinki, Finland (1993–97).

Franklin Israel

Born in 1945 in New York, Franklin Israel was educated at the University of Pennsylvania, Yale and Columbia. He received the Rome Prize in Architecture in 1973, and worked with Giovanni Pasanella in New York, and Llewelyn-Davies, Weeks, Forestier-Walker and Bor in London and Tehran before becoming an art director at Paramount Pictures (1978–79), participating in film projects in Los Angeles, China and the Philippines. He created his own firm, Franklin D. Israel Design Associates, in 1983. His completed projects include offices for Propaganda Films in Hollywood, and Virgin Records in Beverly Hills. Confirming his close connections to the movie industry, he has also designed a Malibu beach house for Robert Altman. Franklin Israel died in 1996.

Philip Johnson

Born in Cleveland, Ohio (1906). Harvard, B.A. (1930), Harvard, B. Arch. (1943). Founder and Director, Department of Architecture, Museum of Modern Art, New York (1932–34, and 1945–54). Wrote *The International Style*, with Henry-Russell Hitchcock (1932) on the occasion of landmark exhibit at MoMA; 1979 Pritzker Prize. Organized 1988 exhibition Deconstructivist Architecture, at MoMA with Mark Wigley. Works: Philip Johnson House, Cambridge, Massachusetts (1942); Philip Johnson House, New Canaan, Connecticut (1949); Seagram Building, New York (with Ludwig Mies van der Rohe), (1958); Boston Public Library, addition (with Architects Design Group), (1973); Pennzoil Place, Houston (1976); AT&T Headquarters Building, New York (1979); PPG Building, Pittsburgh, Pennsylvania (1981); IBM Tower, Atlanta, Georgia (1987); Cathedral of Hope, Dallas, Texas (1996–2000).

Wes Jones

Wes Jones, born in 1958 in Santa Monica, attended the US Military Academy at West Point, the University of California at Berkeley (BA), and the Harvard Graduate School of Design (M. Arch.). A recipient of the Rome Prize in Architecture, he has served as a visiting Professor at Harvard, Rice, Tulane and Columbia Universities. He worked with Eisenman/Robertson, Architects in New York before becoming Director of Design at Holt & Hinshaw in San Francisco. As partner in charge of design at Holt Hinshaw Pfau Jones, he completed the Astronauts' Memorial at Kennedy Space Center in Florida, and the South Campus Chiller Plant for UCLA.

Fumihiko Maki

Born in Tokyo in 1928, Fumihiko Maki received his B. Arch. degree from the University of Tokyo in 1952, and M. Arch. degrees from the Cranbrook Academy of Art (1953) and the Harvard Graduate School of Design (1954). He worked for Skidmore, Owings & Merrill in New York (1954–55) and Sert Jackson and Associates in Cambridge, MA (1955–58) before creating his own firm, Maki and Associates, in Tokyo in 1965. Notable buildings: Fujisawa Municipal Gymnasium, Fujisawa, Kanagawa (1984); Spiral, Minato-ku, Tokyo (1985); National Museum of Modern Art, Sakyo-ku, Kyoto (1986); Tepia, Minato-ku, Tokyo (1989); Nippon Convention Center Makuhari Messe, Chiba, Chiba (1989); Tokyo Metropolitan Gymnasium, Shibuya, Tokyo (1990); and Center for the Arts Yerba Buena Gardens, San Francisco, CA (1993). Current projects include Nippon Convention Center Makuhari Messe Phase II, Chiba, Chiba (1998 completion).

Alessandro Mendini

Born in Milan in 1931, Alessandro Mendini received his doctorate in architecture from the Milan Polytechnic University in 1959. Editor of the magazine *Casabella* from 1970 to 1976, he was a member of the Archizoom and Superstudio groups, and editor of *Modo* from 1977 to 1980, where he defended decorative arts and the value of kitsch. Editor of *Domus* from 1980 to 1985, he created the Domus Academy in 1982. Mendini collaborated with Studio Alchymia from 1979 to 1991, and is the artistic director of Alessi and Swatch. Although Alessandro Mendini has worked on numerous architectural projects such as *La Casa della Felicità* (1980–88), he is best known as a figure of the world of design.

Morphosis

Morphosis principal Thom Mayne, born in Connecticut in 1944, received his B. Arch. in 1968 (USC), and his M. Arch. degree at Harvard in 1978. He created Morphosis in 1979 with Michael Rotondi, who has since left to create his own firm, RoTo. He has taught at UCLA, Harvard, and Yale and SCI-Arc, of which he was a founding Board Member. Based in Santa Monica, CA, some of the main buildings of Morphosis are the Lawrence House (1981); Kate Mantilini Restaurant, Beverly Hills (1986); Cedar's Sinai Comprehensive Cancer Care Center, Beverly Hills (1987); Los Angeles Arts Park, Performing Arts Pavilion, Los Angeles, competition (1989); Crawford Residence, Montecito (1987–92); Yuzen Vintage Car Museum, West Hollywood, project (1992); as well as the more recent Blades Residence (Goleta, 1992–), and projects for schools in California (La Jolla Country Day School, La Jolla, Pomona Unified School District, competition, 1993).

Rem Koolhaas

Rem Koolhaas was born in The Hague in 1944. Before studying at the Architectural Association in London, he tried his hand as a journalist for the *Haagse Post* and as a screenwriter. He founded the Office for Metropolitan Architecture in London in 1975, and became well known after the 1978 publication of his book *Delirious New York*. His built work includes: a group of apartments at Nexus World, Fukuoka (1991); the Villa dall'Ava, Saint-Cloud (1985–91). He was named head architect of the Euralille project in Lille in 1988, and has worked on a design for the new Jussieu University Library in Paris. His recent 1,400-page book *S,M,L,XL* (Monacelli Press, 1995) promises to maintain his reputation as an influential writer.

Richard Meier

Born in Newark, New Jersey in 1934, Richard Meier received his architectural training at Cornell University, and worked in the office of Marcel Breuer (1960–63) before establishing his own practice in 1963. Pritzker Prize, 1984; Royal Gold Medal, 1988. Notable buildings: The Atheneum, New Harmony, IN (1975–79); Museum for the Decorative Arts, Frankfurt, Germany (1979–84); High Museum of Art, Atlanta, GA (1980–83); Canal Plus Headquarters, Paris, France (1988–91); City Hall and Library, The Hague, The Netherlands (1990–95); Barcelona Museum of Contemporary Art, Barcelona, Spain (1988–95); and Getty Center, Los Angeles, CA (1984–96).

Enric Miralles

Born in Barcelona in 1955, Enric Miralles received his degree from the Escuela Técnica Superior de Arquitectura in that city in 1978. He worked with Helio Piñón and Albert Viaplana (1974–84) before forming his partnership with Carme Pinós in 1983. He has lectured at Columbia University in New York, at Harvard, and at the Architectural Association in London. His work includes: the Igualada Cemetery Park on the outskirts of Barcelona (1985–92); the Olympic Archery Ranges, Barcelona (1989–91); the La Mina civic center, Barcelona (1987–92); the Morella Boarding School, Castelló (1986–94); and the Huesca Sports Hall (1988–94).

Eric Owen Moss

Born in Los Angeles, California, in 1943, Eric Owen Moss received his B.A. degree from UCLA in 1965, and his M. Arch. in 1968. He also received a M. Arch. degree at Harvard in 1972. He has been a Professor of Design at the Southern California Institute of Architecture since 1974. He opened his own firm in Culver City in 1976. His built work includes: the Central Housing Office, University of California at Irvine, Irvine (1986–89); Lindblade Tower, Culver City (1987–89); Paramount Laundry, Culver City (1987–89); Gary Group, Culver City (1988–90), The Box, Culver City (1990–94); and the IRS Building, also in Culver City (1993–94).

Jean Nouvel

Born in 1945 in Fumel, Jean Nouvel was admitted to the École des Beaux-Arts in Bordeaux in 1964. In 1970 he created his first office with François Seigneur. His first widely noticed project was the Institut du Monde Arabe in Paris (1981–87, with Architecture Studio). Other recent projects include: his Nemausus housing, Nîmes (1985–87); offices for the CLM/BBDO advertising firm, Issy-les-Moulineaux (1988–92); and his unbuilt projects for the 400 m tall "Tours sans fins", La Défense, Paris (1989); and the Grand Stade for the 1998 World Cup, Paris (1994). Current work includes a store for the Galeries Lafayette, Friedrichstrasse, Berlin, and a project for a cultural center in Lucerne.

Ieoh Ming Pei

Born in 1917 in Canton (now Guangzhou), China, Pei came to the United States in 1935. B. Arch., M.I.T. (1940); M. Arch., Harvard (1942); Doctorate, Harvard (1946). Formed I.M. Pei & Associates, 1955. AIA Gold Medal, 1979; Pritzker Prize, 1983; Praemium Imperiale, Japan, 1989. Notable buildings: National Center for Atmospheric Research, Boulder, CO (1961–67); Federal Aviation Agency Air Traffic Control Towers, fifty buildings, various locations (1962–70); John F. Kennedy Library, Boston, MA (1965–79); National Gallery of Art, East Building, Washington, D.C. (1968–78); Bank of China Tower, Hong Kong (1982–89); Grand Louvre, Paris (1983–93); and Rock and Roll Hall of Fame, Cleveland, OH (1993–95). Current projects include a museum for Shinji Shumeikai, Shiga, Japan.

Cesar Pelli

Born in 1926 in Tucuman, Argentina, studied at Tucuman University, Dip. Arch. (1949). Emigrated to the U.S. (1952) and attended University of Illinois, M. Arch. (1954). Worked in office of Eero Saarinen and Associates, Bloomfield Hills, MI, and New Haven, CT (1954–64); project designer for the TWA Terminal, Kennedy International Airport, New York, and Vivian Beaumont Theater at Lincoln Center, New York. In 1964, joined DMJM, Los Angeles, as director (1964–66), then vice-president of design (1966–68). From 1968 to 1977, Pelli was partner in charge of design at Gruen Associates, Los Angeles. Notable buildings completed by Gruen Associates under Pelli's direction include: the Pacific Design Center in Los Angeles (1975) and U.S. Embassy in Tokyo, Japan (1976). After becoming Dean of the School of Architecture at Yale in 1977, Pelli opened his own office, Cesar Pelli and Associates, in New Haven, CT. Notable structures include: Residential tower and gallery expansion, Museum of Modern Art, NY (1977); Four Leaf Towers, Houston, TX (1983–85); World Financial Center, NY (1980–88); Canary Wharf Tower, London (1987–91); NTT Shinjuku Headquarters Building, Tokyo, Japan (1990–95); and Kuala Lumpur City Centre Phase 1, Malaysia (1992–96).

Dominique Perrault

Dominique Perrault was born in 1953 in Clermont-Ferrand, France. He received his diploma as an architect from the Beaux-Arts UP 6 in Paris in 1978. He received a further degree in urbanism at the École nationale des Ponts et Chaussées, Paris, in 1979. He created his own firm in 1981 in Paris. Built work includes: the Engineering School (ESIEE) in Marne-la-Vallée (1984–87); the Hôtel industriel Jean-Baptiste Berlier, Paris (1986–90); the Hôtel du département de la Meuse, Bar-le-Duc, France (1988–94); and the Bibliothèque nationale de France, Paris (1989–96). Current work includes: the Olympic Velodrome, swimming and diving pool, Berlin, Germany (1992–98); and a large-scale study of the urbanism of Bordeaux (1992–2000).

Renzo Piano

Born in 1937 in Genoa, Renzo Piano studied at the University of Florence and at the Polytechnic Institute in Milan. He formed his own practice (Studio Piano) in the 1960s, then associated with Richard Rogers (Piano & Rogers, 1971–78). They completed the Pompidou Center in Paris in 1977. From 1978 to 1980, Piano worked with Peter Rice (Piano & Rice Associates). He created the Renzo Piano Building Workshop in 1981 in Genoa and Paris. His work includes: the Menil Collection Museum, Houston (1986); the San Nicola stadium, Bari (1987–90); the 1989 extension for the IRCAM, Paris; and the renovation of the Lingotto complex, Turin. Current work includes the center for Kanak Culture, Noumea, and projects near the Potsdamer Platz in Berlin.

Christian de Portzamparc

Born in Casablanca in 1944, Christian de Portzamparc studied at the École des Beaux Arts in Paris from 1962 to 1969. Early projects include a water tower in Marne-la-Vallée (1971–74); and the Hautes Formes public housing, Paris (1975–79). He won the competition for the Cité de la Musique on the outskirts of Paris in 1984, completing the project in 1995. He was awarded the 1994 Pritzker Prize. He participated in the Euralille project with a tower built over the new Lille-Europe railway station in Lille, and built housing for the Nexus World project in Fukuoka (1992). Current work includes an addition to the Palais des Congrès in Paris, a tower for the Bandai toy company in Tokyo, and a courthouse for Grasse in the south of France.

Antoine Predock

Born in 1936 in Lebanon, Missouri; educated at the University of New Mexico and Columbia University, B. Arch. 1962. Antoine Predock has been the principal of his own firm since 1967. He has taught at UCLA and California State Polytechnic University. Notable buildings: Nelson Fine Arts Center, Arizona State University, Tempe, AZ (1986–89); Zuber House, Phoenix, AZ (1986–89); Hotel Santa Fe, Disneyland Paris, Marne-la-Vallée, France (1990–92); Classroom/Laboratory/Administration Building, California Polytechnic University, Pomona, CA (1993); American Heritage Center, Laramie, WY (1987–93); Civic Arts Plaza, Thousand Oaks, CA (1989-94); and Ventana Vista Elementary School, Tucson, AZ (1992–94).

Bart Prince

Born in Albuquerque, NM, in 1947. B. Arch., Arizona State University (1970). Worked with Bruce Goff from 1968 to 1973, assisted him in the design of the Pavilion for Japanese Art, Los Angeles County Museum of Art, Los Angeles, CA (1978–89), and completed the building after Goff's death in 1982. Opened his own architectural practice in 1973. Main buildings: Bart Prince Residence and studio, Albuquerque, NM (1983); Joe Price Residence, Corona del Mar, CA (1986); Brad and June Prince House, Albuquerque, NM (1988); Nollan Residence, Taos, NM (1993); Mead/Penhall Residence, Albuquerque, NM (1994); and Hight Residence, Mendocino County, CA (1995).

Aldo Rossi

Aldo Rossi was born in Milan in 1931. Began studies at Milan Polytechnic, 1949. Began working with Ernesto Rogers on the architecture magazine *Casabella-Continuità* in 1956. Graduated from Milan Polytechnic, 1959. Editor of *Casabella-Continuità*, 1964. His 1966 book *Architecture and the City* is considered a significant study of urban design and thinking. Appointed professor at Milan Polytechnic 1965; professor at Federal Polytechnic of Zurich, 1972; University of Venice, 1973. 1990 Pritzker Prize. Significant work includes: Cemetary of San Cataldo, Modena, Italy (1971–90); Teatro del Mondo, Venice, Italy, Venice Biennale (1980); Südliche Friedrichstadt Housing Complex, Berlin, Germany (1981–88); Centro Torri Commercial Center, Parma, Italy (1985–88); Il Palazzo Hotel, Fukuoka, Japan (1989); Modern Art Museum, Vassivière, Limousin, France (1988–90); and Office Tower, Mexico City, Mexico (1994–, in progress).

Schneider + Schumacher

Till Schneider, born in 1959, studied at the University of Kaiserslautern. Received diploma from the Technische Hochschule, Darmstadt. Postgraduate studies at the Staatliche Hochschule für Bildende Künste, Städelschule, Frankfurt, in the class of Peter Cook. Worked in offices of Eisele + Fritz, Darmstadt, and Robert Mürb, Karlsruhe. Created his own office in Frankfurt with Michael Schumacher (1988). Michael Schumacher, born in 1957, also studied at University of Kaiserslautern. Postgraduate studies at the Staatliche Hochschule für Bildende Künste, Städelschule, Frankfurt, in the class of Peter Cook. Worked in the office of Norman Foster, London, and Braun & Schlockermann, Frankfurt, before 1988. Most important built work: office building for J. Walter Thompson, Frankfurt (1994–95). Most important current job: administrative building for KPMG (Deutsche Treuhandgesellschaft), in Leipzig, scheduled for mid-1997 completion.

SITE

James Wines, founding principal of SITE (Sculpture in the Environment) was born in Chicago, IL, and studied art and art history at Syracuse University, BA 1956. Between 1965 and 1967 he was a sculptor. He created SITE with Alison Sky and Michelle Stone in 1970. Notable buildings include: Indeterminate Facade Showroom, Houston, TX (1975); Ghost Parking Lot, Hamden, CT (1978); Highway 86, World Exposition, Vancouver, British Columbia, Canada (1986); Four Continents Bridge, Hiroshima, Japan (1989); Avenida 5, Universal Exhibition, Seville, Spain (1992); and Ross's Landing Plaza and Park, Chattanooga, TN (1992).

Sir Richard Rogers

Born in Florence, Italy, of British parents in 1933, Richard Rogers studied at the Architectural Association in London (1954–59). He received his M. Arch. degree from the Yale University School of Architecture in 1962. Created partnerships with his wife Su Rogers, Norman and Wendy Foster (Team 4, London, 1964–66); and with Renzo Piano in London, Paris and Genoa (1971–77). He created Richard Rogers Partnership in London (1977). He has taught at Yale, and has been Chairman of the Trustees of the Tate Gallery, London (1981–89). Main buildings include: the Centre Georges Pompidou, Paris (with Renzo Piano, 1971–77); Lloyd's of London, headquarters (1978–86); Channel 4 television headquarters, London (1990–94); Daimler Benz office building, Potsdamer Platz, Berlin (1994–); and Bordeaux Palais de Justice (1993–).

Michael Rotondi

Born in 1949 in Los Angeles, Michael Rotondi received his B. Arch. from the Southern California Institute of Architecture (SCI-Arc) in 1973. He worked with DMJM in Los Angeles (1973–76), and collaborated with Peter de Bretteville and Craig Hodgetts from 1974 to 1976. He was Director of the Graduate Design Faculty at SCI-Arc from 1976 to 1987. Founding principal of Morphosis with Thom Mayne, Michael Rotondi has been the Director of SCI-Arc since 1987. He left Morphosis in 1991 and created his present firm, RoTo, in 1993. Ongoing projects include the Nicola Restaurant (Los Angeles); CDLT 1,2, Cedar Lodge Terrace, Silverlake (started in 1989); and the Qwfk House. A recently designed project is Warehouse C, a 210 m long structure to be built on landfill in the harbor of Nagasaki, Japan.

Josh Schweitzer

Born in 1953 in Cincinnati, Ohio, Josh Schweitzer (B.A., Pitzer College, Claremont, CA; M. Arch., University of Kansas, 1980), worked for Spence + Webster in London, PBNA in Kansas City, and Frank O. Gehry in Santa Monica, before creating his own partnership, Schweitzer-Kellen in 1984, and his own office, Schweitzer BIM, opened in 1987. Besides The Monument, his completed work includes restaurants such as Venue, Kansas City (1993), or the California Chicken Café, Los Angeles (1992). He recently completed the Big Life Sports Bar in Fukuoka, Japan, and has begun work on a 450 ha Water Park/Hotel complex in southern Japan. Also recently completed, the Mossimo sportswear store at South Coast Plaza (Costa Mesa, CA).

Alvaro Siza

Born in Matosinhos, Portugal, in 1933, Alvaro Siza studied at the University of Porto School of Architecture (1949–55). He created his own practice in 1954, and worked with Fernando Tavora from 1955 to 1958. He has been a Professor of Construction at the University of Porto since 1976. He received the European Community's Mies van der Rohe Prize in 1988 and the Pritzker Prize in 1992. He built a large number of small-scale projects in Portugal, and more recently he has worked on the restructuring of the Chiado, Lisbon, Portugal (1989–); the Meteorology Center, Barcelona, Spain (1989–92); the Vitra Furniture Factory, Weil am Rhein, Germany (1991–94); the Oporto School of Architecture, Oporto University (1986–95); and the University of Aveiro Library, Aveiro, Portugal (1988–95).

Otto Steidle

Born in Munich in 1943, Otto Steidle studied at the Akademie der Bildenden Künste in that city from 1965 to 1969. In 1966, he created the firm Muhr + Steidle, and in 1969 Steidle + Partner. He has taught extensively, in Munich, Kassel, Berlin, Amsterdam and at MIT in Cambridge, Massachusetts (1991,1993). He has been Rector of the Munich Akademie der Bildenden Künste since 1993. Built work includes housing on the Genter Strasse in Munich, where he has his offices (1969–75); the Kreuzgassen Quarter, Nuremberg (1986–92); and the headquarters of Gruner + Jahr, Hamburg (1983–91). Work under construction includes a residential and commercial building, Landshut, and the Pensions Fund Building of the Wacker Chemie Corporation in Munich.

Simon Ungers

Born in 1957 in Cologne, Germany, emmigrated to the United States in 1979. B. Arch., Cornell 1979. Founding partner of UKZ (1981); Assistant Professor of Architecture at Syracuse University, New York, 1981–86. Hobbs Residence, Lansing, NY, 1982; Honorable Mention, Japan Opera House Competition, 1986; Assistant Professor of Architecture at Rensselaer Polytechnic Institute (1986–1992). Numerous installations: Gallery Sophia Ungers, Cologne, Germany, 1993; Sandra Gering Gallery, New York, 1992. 1995 First Prize in Holocaust Memorial Competition, Berlin, Germany.

Shin Takamatsu

Born in Shimane Prefecture in 1948, Shin Takamatsu graduated from Kyoto University in 1971 and from the Graduate School of the same institution in 1979. After working with Kiyoshi Kawasaki from 1971 to 1975, he created his own office in Kyoto in 1975. He has taught at Kyoto Technical University and at the Osaka University of Arts. Profiting amply from the building boom of the 1980s, Takamatsu completed a large number of structures including: Origin I, II and III (Kamigyo, Kyoto, 1980–86); the Kirin Plaza, Chuo, Osaka (1985–87); and Syntax, Sakyo-ku, Kyoto (1988–90). In his more recent, less mechanical style, Takamatsu has completed the Kirin Headquarters, Chuo-ku, Tokyo (1993–95); the Shoji Ueda Museum of Photography, Kishimoto-cho, Tottori (1993–95); and the Nagasaki Port Terminal Building, Motofune-cho, Nagasaki (1994–95).

Valode & Pistre

Denis Valode was born in 1946, and was a professor of architecture at the École des Beaux Arts (UP1 and UP2) from 1972 to 1985. Jean Pistre was born in 1951. They first worked together in 1977 and established their office Valode & Pistre in 1980. Built work includes the renovation of the CAPC, Bordeaux (1990); the installation of the Direction régionale des Affaires Culturelles (Regional Cultural Authority) in an eighteenth century building, Lyon (1987–92); CFDT Headquarters, Paris (1986–90); Shell Headquarters, Reuil-Malmaison, France (1988–91); EPS Schlumberger, Clamart (1989–93); Leonardo da Vinci University, Courbevoie, France (1992–95); Air France Headquarters, Roissy Airport (1992–95). Outside of France, they have worked on a planned Media Tower, Babelsberg, Potsdam (1993), and offices and a hotel also for Potsdam (1993).

BIBLIOGRAPHY

"Architects in Cyberspace", *Architectural Design Profile* n° 118. Academy Group, London, 1995.

"Architecture of Transportation", *Architectural Design*. London, 1994.

Architectures of Herzog & de Meuron. Peter Blum Edition, New York, 1994.

Architektur Jahrbuch, 1992, 1993, 1994. Prestel, München.

Art and Power, Europe under the Dictators, 1930–45. Hayward Gallery, 1995.

Asymptote, Architecture at the Interval. Rizzoli, New York, 1995.

Banham, Reyner and Hiroyuki Suzuki: *Contemporary Architecture of Japan 1958–1984*. Architectural Press, London, 1985.

Bédard, Jean–François (ed.): *Cities of Artificial Excavation, The Work of Peter Eisenman, 1978–1988*. Rizzoli International, Singapore, 1994.

"Ben van Berkel", *El Croquis*, 72(I). Madrid, 1995.

Berlin, World Cities. Academy Editions, London, 1995.

Bertoni, Franco: *Philippe Starck, L'architecture*. Mardaga, Liège, 1994.

Betsky, Aaron: *Violated Perfection, Architecture and the Fragmentation of the Modern*. Rizzoli, New York, 1990.

Bibliothèque Nationale de France 1989–1995. Artemis, Zurich, 1995.

Binney, Marcus: *Architecture of Rail, The Way Ahead*. Academy Editions, London, 1995.

Bouman, Ole: *The Invisible in Architecture*. Academy Editions, London, 1994.

Buchanan, Peter: *Renzo Piano Building Workshop*, Complete Works, Volume 1. Phaidon Press, London, 1994.

Buchanan, Peter: *Renzo Piano Building Workshop*, Complete Works, Volume 2. Phaidon Press, London, 1995.

Collins, Brad and Juliette Robbins (compiled by): *Antoine Predock, Architect*. Rizzoli, New York, 1994.

Cook, Peter and George Rand: *Morphosis, Buildings and Projects*. Rizzoli, New York, 1989.

Crosbie, Michael (introduction): *Cesar Pelli, Images Publishing*. Mulgrave, Australia, 1993.

Cullen, Michael: *Calatrava Berlin, 5 Projects*. Birkhäuser, Berlin, 1994.

Cultural Facilities, New Concepts in Architecture & Design. Meisei Publications, Tokyo, 1993.

Davidson, Cynthia (ed.): *Architecture beyond Architecture. Creativity and Social Transformations in Islamic Architecture. The 1995 Aga Khan Award for Architecture*. Academy Editions, London, 1995.

Dietsch, Deborah: "Philip's Folly", *Architecture*. November 1995.

Dixon, John Morris: "The Santa Monica School. What's Its Lasting Contribution?" *Progressive Architecture*. May 1995.

Dixon, John Morris: "Superstructure", *Progressive Architecture*, July 1995.

Dos Santos, José Paulo (ed.): *Alvaro Siza, Works & Projects 1954–1992*. Gustavo Gili, Barcelona, 1993.

Emanuel, Muriel (ed.): *Contemporary Architects*. St James Press, New York, 3rd edition, 1994.

Escher, Frank (ed.): *John Lautner, Architect*. Artemis, 1994.

Feireiss, Kristin (ed.): *Ben van Berkel, Mobile Forces*. Ernst & Sohn, Berlin, 1994.

Feldmeyer, Gerhard: *The New German Architecture*. Rizzoli, New York, 1993.

Foster, Norman: *Sir Norman Foster and Partners*. Sir Norman Foster and Partners Publications, London, 1993.

Frampton, Kenneth (introduction): essay by Fréderic Migayrou, Steven Holl. Artemis, Zürich, 1994.

Frampton, Kenneth: *Tadao Ando*. The Museum of Modern Art, New York, 1991.

Frampton, Kenneth and Joseph Rykwert: *Richard Meier Architect, 1985/1991*. Rizzoli, New York, 1991.

Frampton, Kenneth, Charles Jencks and Richard Meier: *Richard Meier, Buildings and Projects, 1979–1989*. St Martin's Press, New York, 1990.

Massimiliano Fuksas. Artemis, Zurich, 1994.

Futagawa, Yukio (ed.): "Frank O. Gehry", *GA Architect* n°10. A.D.A. Edita, Tokyo, 1993.

Futagawa, Yukio (ed.): "Steven Holl", *GA Architect* n°11. A.D.A. Edita, Tokyo, 1993.

Futagawa, Yukio (ed.): "Hiroshi Hara", *GA Architect* n°13. A.D.A. Edita, Tokyo, 1993.

Futagawa, Yukio (ed.): "Tadao Ando", *GA Document* Extra 01. A.D.A. Edita, Tokyo, 1995.

Futagawa, Yukio (ed.): "Richard Rogers", *GA Document* Extra 02. A.D.A. Edita, Tokyo, 1995.

Futagawa, Yukio (ed.): "Zaha Hadid", *GA Document* Extra 03. A.D.A. Edita, Tokyo, 1995.

Galloway, David: *Richard Meier, Stadthaus Ulm*. International Creative Management, Niederstatzingen, 1993.

Gares 1994, La nouvelle génération. SNCF, Paris, 1994.

Gebhard, David and Robert Winter: *Los Angeles, An Architectural Guide*. Gibbs–Smith, Salt Lake City, 1994.

"Frank O. Gehry", *El Croquis*, 74/75. Madrid, 1995.

Ghiradro, Diane: "Eisenman's Bogus Avant-Garde", *Progressive Architecture*. November 1994.

Glancey, Jonathan: "Ideas beyond the nuclear station", *The Independent*. April 12, 1995

Goldberger, Paul: "The Masterpieces They Call Home", *The New York Times Magazine*, March 12, 1995.

Goldberger, Paul: *The Skyscraper*. Alfred A. Knopf, New York, 1981.

Goulet, Patrice: *Jean Nouvel*. Éditions du Regard, Paris, 1994.

"Zaha Hadid", *El Croquis*, 73(I). Madrid, 1995.

"Itsuko Hasegawa", *Architectural Monographs*, n°31. Academy Editions, London, 1993.

Hines, Thomas: *Richard Neutra and the Search for Modern Architecture*. University of California Press, Berkeley, 1994.

Hitchcock, Henry–Russell and Philip Johnson: *The International Style*. W.W. Norton & Company, New York, 1932.

"Franklin D. Israel", *Architectural Monographs* n°34. Academy Editions, London, 1994.

Israel, Franklin D. and Thomas Hines: *Franklin D. Israel*. Rizzoli, New York, 1992.

"Toyo Ito", *JA Library 2*. Summer 1993, Shinkenchiku–sha Co., Ltd., Tokyo.

Jencks, Charles (ed.): *Frank O. Gehry, Individual Imagination and Cultural Conservatism*. Academy Editions, London, 1995.

Jencks, Charles: *Heteropolis, Los Angeles, the Riots and the Strange Beauty of Hetero-Architecture*. Academy Editions, London, 1993.

Johnson, Philip and Mark Wigley: *Deconstructivist Architecture*. The Museum of Modern Art, New York, 1988.

Johnson, Philip (foreword): *Arquitectonica*. American Institute of Architects Press, Washington, D.C., 1991.

Kabakov, Ilya: *Installations 1983–1995*. Centre Georges Pompidou, Paris, 1995.

"Kansai International Airport Passenger Terminal Building", *The Japan Architect* n°15. Autumn 1994.

Kaplan, Sam Hall: *LA Lost & Found*. Crown Trade Paperbacks, New York, 1987.

Koolhaas, Rem: *Delirious New York*. The Monacelli Press, New York, 1994, originally published in 1978.

Koolhaas, Rem: *S, M, L, XL*. The Monacelli Press, New York, 1995.

Koshalek, Richard (preface): *Arata Isozaki, Architecture 1960 – 1990*. The Museum of Contemporary Art, Los Angeles, Rizzoli, New York, 1991.

Lacy, Bill (ed.): *Angels and Franciscans, Innovative Architecture from Los Angeles and San Francisco*. Rizzoli, New York, 1992.

Le Dantec, Jean-Pierre: *Christian de Portzamparc*. Éditions du Regard, Paris, 1995.

"Lignes étirées, Université des Sciences à Ulm, Allemagne", *Techniques & Architecture*, octobre–novembre 1992.

London, World Cities. Academy Editions, London, 1993.

Los Angeles, World Cities. Academy Editions, London, 1994.

"Los Angeles, 1994", *Abitare*, n° 329, May 1994.

Machado, Rodolfo and Rodolphe El–Khoury: *Monolithic Architecture*. The Heinz Architectural Center, The Carnegie Museum of Art, Pittsburgh, Prestel, Munich, 1995.

"Fumihiko Maki", *The Japan Architect*, n° 16, Winter 1994, Shinkenchiku-sha Co., Ltd., Tokyo.

McGrew, Patrick and Robert Julian: *Landmarks of Los Angeles*. Harry Abrams, New York, 1994.

Meier, Richard (foreword by Joseph Rykwert): *Richard Meier Architect, 1964/1984*. Rizzoli, New York, 1984.

Meier, Richard and Frank Stella: *Arte et Architettura*, Exhibition catalogue, Rome, Palazzo delle Esposizioni, 8 July – 30 August 1993. Electa, Milan, 1993.

Mierop, Caroline: *Gratte-Ciel*. Éditions Norma, Paris, 1995.

"Enric Miralles", *El Croquis*, 72(II). Madrid, 1995.

"Enric Miralles", *Architectural Monographs* n° 10. Academy Editions, London, 1995.

"Eric Owen Moss, 1974 – 1994", *Architecture and Urbanism* (A+U), 94:11.

Eric Owen Moss, Buildings and Projects. Rizzoli, New York, 1991.

"Eric Owen Moss", *Architectural Monographs* n° 20. Academy Editions, London, 1993.

Muschamp, Herbert: "A Flare for Fantasy: 'Miami Vice' Meets 42nd Street", *The New York Times*. May 21, 1995 .

Muschamp, Herbert: "Building on the Ruins of Temples to Nuclear Power", *The New York Times*, April 2, 1995.

Muschamp, Herbert: "Rem Koolhaas's New York State of Mind", *The New York Times*, November 4, 1994.

Nitschke, Günther: *From Shinto to Ando*. Academy Editions, London, 1993.

Noever, Peter (ed.): *Architecture in Transition, Between Deconstruction and New Modernism*. Prestel, Munich, 1993.

Noever, Peter (ed.): *The End of Architecture?* Prestel, Munich, 1993.

Dominique Perrault. Artemis, Zurich, 1994.

Polledri, Paolo (ed.): *Visionary San Francisco*. Prestel, Munich, 1990.

Petit, Jean: *Botta, traces d'architecture*. Fidia Edizioni d'Arte, Lugano, 1994.

"Reaching for the Skies", *Architectural Design Profile* n° 116, Academy Group, London, 1995.

Reichstag Berlin. Aedes, Berlin, 1994.

Rice, Peter: *An Engineer Imagines*. Artemis, Zurich, 1994.

Saliga, Pauline and Martha Thorne: *Building in a New Spain*. Editorial Gustavo Gili, Bacelona, 1992.

Siza, Alvaro: *Works and Projects*. Electa Espana, 1995.

Smith, C. Ray: *Supermannerism*. E.P. Dutton, New York, 1977.

SOM, Architecture of Skidmore, Owings & Merrill, 1984–1994. Images Publishing, Mulgrave, Australia, 1995.

Steele, James: *Los Angeles Architecture, The Contemporary Condition*. Phaidon Press, London, 1993.

Steele, James: *Eames House, Charles and Ray Eames*. Phaidon, London, 1994.

Steidle, Otto: *Bewohnbare Bauten*. Artemis, Zürich, 1994.

Sudjic, Deyan: *The architecture of Richard Rogers*. Wordsearch, London, 1994.

"Tensile Structures", *A.D. Architectural Design*. London, 1995.

Tzonis, Alexander and Liane Lefaivre: *Architecture in Europe since 1968*. Thames & Hudson, London, 1992.

Tzonis, Alexander and Liane Lefaivre: *Movement, Structure and the Work of Santiago Calatrava*. Birkhäuser, Basel, 1995.

Venturi, Robert: *Complexity and Contradiction in Architecture*. The Museum of Modern Art, New York, 1966.

Weinstein, Richard: *Morphosis, Buildings and Projects, 1989–1992*. Rizzoli, New York, 1994.

Wiseman, Carter: *I.M. Pei, A Profile in American Architecture*. Harry N. Abrams, Inc., New York, 1990.

Williams, Harold, Bill Lacy, Stephen Rountree and Richard Meier: *The Getty Center, Design Process*. The J. Paul Getty Trust, Los Angeles, 1991.

Woods, Lebbeus: *The New City*. Simon & Schuster, New York, 1992.

Woods, Lebbeus: *War and Architecture*. Pamphlet Architecture 15, Princeton Architectural Press, New York, 1993.

INDEX

Aalto, Alvar 224
Acconci, Vito 71, 100
Ando, Tadao 42, 78, **78, 79**, 88, 92, 93, **93**, 99, 111, 112, 114, **112–114**, 116, 130, 132, 174, 175, **179**, 181, 182, **182, 183**, 220, 227
Andreu, Paul 54
Arakawa, Shusaku 94, 95
Architecture Studio 38, 40, **40, 41**, 227, 231
Arquitectonica 62, 63, **63**, 64, 227
Arup Associates 205
Asymptote 36, **36, 37**, 227
Atelier φ 228
Berkel, Ben van 71
Beuys, Joseph 149
Birkerts, Gunnar 126, 227
Bofill, Ricardo 54
Böhm, Gottfried 28
Boltanski, Christian **90**
Botta, Mario 99, **99**, 100, **101**, 116, 120, **120, 121**, 136, 138, **138**, 227
Brancusi, Constantin 134
Breuer, Marcel 181, 182, 230
Bruder, Will 107, 124, **124, 125**, 126, 227
Bruggen, Coosje van 158, 159
Buren, Daniel 148, **148, 149**
Calatrava, Santiago 38, 60, 61, **60, 61**, 78, 228
Calder, Alexander 145
Christo & Jeanne-Claude 144, 145, 146, **146, 147**, 148
Coop Himmelblau 8, 20, 22, **24**, 25, 26, **27**, 40, 86, 163, 168, 190
Couture, Lise Anne 36, 37, 227
Duthilleul, Jean-Marie 14, 38, 56, 57, **56, 57**, 116
Egeraat, Erick van 208, 210, **210, 211**, 228
Eiffel, Gustave 59
Eisenman, Peter 8, 12, 13, 14, 18, **18, 19**, 20, 37, 67, 188, 189, **188, 189**, 194, 198, 228, 230
Fontana, Lucio 111, 128
Fort-Brescia, Bernardo 63, 227
Foster, Sir Norman 53, 54, 56, 60, 62, **62**, 84, 86, **86, 87**, 145, 208, **209**, 213, 228, 232
Freed, James 100
Fuksas, Massimiliano **109, 110**, 111, 126, **126, 127**, 128, 148, 149, 150, **151**, 228
Fuller, Richard Buckminster 135, 181, 219, 228
Fung, Hsin-Ming 77, 229
Gaudí, Antoni 60, 150
Gehry, Frank O. 8, 9, 10, **10, 11**, 12, **12**, 13, 28, 44, 81, 83, 84, 85, **88, 89**, 89, 99, 111, 112, 126, 139, **139**, 158, 159, 160, **159, 160**,

161, 162, 189, 190, **190–193**, 193, 198, 208, 220, 228, 232
Goff, Bruce 232
Gonzalez, Julio 145
Graham, Dan 158, 160, **160**
Graves, Michael 62, 188, 198
Gregotti, Vittorio 136
Grimshaw, Nicholas 58, 59, **58, 59**, 111, 219, 220, 228
Hadid, Zaha 8, 10, 13, **13**, 20, 62, 111, 168, 198, 219, 220
Hara, Hiroshi 64, **64, 65**, 68, 212, 228
Hasegawa, Itsuko 42, 44, **43–45**, 128, 132, **132, 133**, 182, 184, **184, 185**, 229
Herzog & de Meuron 88, 90, 92, **92**, 229
HLW International 68, 69, **68, 69**
Hockney, David 158, 162, 163, **162, 163**
Hodgetts + Fung 74, **74, 75**, 77, 128, 229
Hodgetts, Craig 77, 229, 232
Holl, Steven 71, 72, **71–73**, 76, 100, 126, 154, 168, **180**, 181, 193, 194, **194**, 229
Hollein, Hans 28, 84, 85, 90, **90, 91**
Holt Hinshaw Pfau Jones 196, **197**, 197, 199, 230
Ishii, Kazuhiro 54
Isozaki, Arata 42, 84, 93, 94, 95, 96, **95–97**, 111, 132, 134, **134**, 135, 136, 139, 174, 175, 190, 229
Israel, Franklin 100, **102–103**, 103, 229
Ito, Toyo 42, 46, 47, **46, 47**, 93, 94, **94**, 128, 182, 184, 229
Jackson, Sert 230
Johns, Jasper 9
Johnson, Philip 3, 8, 20, 36, 194, **195**, 198, 199, 229
Jones Partners-Architecture 199
Jones, Wes 197, 198, 199, 230
Judd, Donald 154
Kabakov, Ilya 149, 152, **152**, 154
Kahn, Louis 227
Kawamata, Tadashi 173, **173**, 174
Kawasaki, Kiyoshi 233
Kienholz, Ed 9
Kikutake, Kiyonori 54, 174, 175, 229
Kinslow, Tom 165, 171, **171**
Koch, Paul 208
Kohn Pederson Fox 68
Koolhaas, Rem 8, 10, 12, 14, 16, **14–17**, 20, 57, 58, 88, 116, 182, 230
Kuramata, Shiro 216, 218
Kurokawa, Kisho 181
Le Corbusier 124, 227
Le Nôtre, André 83
Libeskind, Daniel 8, 20

Lin, Maya 161, 162, **164**, 165
Lucchi, Michele de 22
Maki, Fumihiko 42, 44, 49. **48, 49**, 94, 98, **98**, 99, 107, 112, 113, 115, 116, **115–117**, 136, 138, **138**, 184, 230
Mayne, Thom 28, 36, 162, 168, 200, 230, 232
Mecanoo 208, 228
Meier, Richard 7, 8, **8, 9**, 12, 84, 90, 111, 113, 116, **118, 119**, 119, 138, 139, 163, 164, 188, 220, 222, 230
Mendini, Alessandro 20, 22, 25, 26, **22–27**, 40, 86, 156, 230
Mies van der Rohe, Ludwig 13
Milunic, Vladimir 208
Miralles, Enric 5, 150, **150**, 154, 209, 212, **212**, 230
Miyake, Issey **52**, 53, 174, 175
Miyawaki, Aiko 94, 96
Moneo, Rafael 78, 88
Moore, Charles 99
Morphosis 28, **29**, 199, 200, 230, 232
Moss, Eric Owen 28, 30, 33, 34, **30–35**, 36, 37, 168, 198, 199, 200, 201, **198–201**, 230
Mulligan, Matt 148
Nervi, Pier Luigi 61, 63, 181, 182
Noguchi, Isamu 134, 174, **174**, 175, 182
Nouvel, Jean 12, 14, 38, 54, 84, 116, 140, **140, 141**, 148, 208, 227, 231
Office for Metropolitan Architecture (OMA) 58, 116, 230
Okazaki, Kazuo 94
Oldenburg, Claes 9, 158, 159
Paxton, Joseph 59
Pei, Ieoh Ming 38, 54, 71, **82, 83**, 84, **84, 85**, 100, 104, **104**, 135, 174, 175, 177, **177**, 231
Pelli, Cesar 64, 66, **66**, 231
Perrault, Dominique 123, **123**, 124, 154, 156, 231
Piano, Renzo 53, 54, **54, 55**, 88, 213, 231, 232
Picasso, Pablo 145
Pinós, Carme 168, 230
Polshek, James Stewart 136
Portzamparc, Christian de 12, 14, 20, 38, **38, 39**, 57, 116, 118, 122, **122**, 136, 137, **137**, 209, 212, 231
Predock, Antoine 104, 105, 107, **105–107**, 126, 231
Prince, Bart 202, **202, 203**, 232
Rashid, Hani 36, 37, 227
Rauschenberg, Bob 9
Raynaud, Jean-Pierre 153, 154, **153–155**, 156
Rheinsberg, Raffael 175, **175**
Rice, Peter 224, 231

Rivera, Diego 145
Rogers, Sir Richard 212, 213, 215, **213–215**, 228, 231, 232
Rokkaku, Kijo 130, 131, **131**
Rossi, Aldo 84, 216, **216, 217**, 218, 229, 232
RoTo 28, 162, 165, **165**, 230
Rotondi, Michael 28, 162, 200, 230, 232
Ruskin, John 145
Sacconi, Anna Maria 228
Saarinen, Eero 38, 53, 63, 231
Schindler, Rudolph 163
Schneider + Schumacher 51, 53, 76, **76, 77**, 78, 219, 232
Schweitzer BIM 166, **166, 167**, 232
Schweitzer, Josh 163, 166, 199, 232
Schwitters, Kurt 10
Sekkei, Nikken 54
Serra, Richard 124, 154, 165, 181
Sert, Josep Lluis 145
Shinohara, Kazuo 128, 129, **129**, 130, 184, 229
SITE **204–207**, 205, 206, 232
Siza, Alvaro 84, 111, **218, 219**, 219, 220, 232
Skidmore, Owings & Merrill (SOM) 68, 70, **70**, 230
Smith, Frederick Norton 33, 200, 201
Soleri, Paolo 126, 227
Sottsass, Ettore 218
Spear, Laurinda Hope 63, 227
Speer, Albert 145
Starck, Philippe **6**, 7, 22, 25, 26, **25, 26**, 38, 40, 41, **41**, 86, 156, **157**, 176, 177, **177**
Steidle, Otto 220, **220, 221**, 222, 233
Stella, Frank 20, 26, **143**, 145, 163, 164, 168, 169, **168, 169**, 198
Stevens, Clark 162
Stirling, James 28, 84
Takamatsu, Shin 175, 176, **176**, 184, 186, **186, 187**, 233
Tange, Kenzo 136, 174, 229
Tatlin, Vladimir 37
Teshigahara, Hiroshi 174, 175, **175**
Teshigahara, Sofu 174
Tschumi, Bernard 8, 14, 20, **20, 21**, 54, 156
Ungers, Oswald Matthias 90
Ungers, Simon 165, 171, **170–171**, 233
Valode & Pistre 222, 223, 224, **222–225**, 233
Vasconi, Claude 57, 116
Venturi, Robert 7, 8
Viñoly, Rafael 135, **135**
Von Gerkan, Marg and Partner 77
Watanabe, Makoto Sei 128, 130, **130**
Wigley, Mark 8, 20, 229
Wines, James 205, 232
Woods, Lebbeus 165, 168, 172, **172**
Yeang, Ken 67, **67**, 68

CREDITS

l. = left / r. = right
t. = top / c. = center / b. = bottom

3   © Photo: 1995
        Norman McGrath
5   © Enric Miralles
6   © Philippe Starck
8   © J. Paul Getty Trust/
        Photo: John Stephens
9   © J. Paul Getty Trust/
        Photo: Scott Frances/Esto
10   © Photo: Richard Bryant/
        Vitra
11   © Photo: Ian McKinnell
12   © Photo: Karin Heßmann
13   © Photo: Richard Bryant/
        Vitra
14–17   © Photo: Ralph Richter/
        Architekturphoto
18 l.   © Eisenman Architects
18 r.   © Jochen Littkemann
19   © Eisenman Architects
20/21   © Photo: Alfred Wolf
22–27   © Photo: Ralph Richter/
        Architekturphoto
29–31   © Photo: Arnaud
        Carpentier
32/33 t. © Photo: Tom Bonner
33 b.   © Eric Owen Moss
34/35   © Photo: Tom Bonner
36/37   © Photo: Asymptote
        Architecture
38/39   © Christian de Portzamparc
40–41   © Photo: Urquijo/Rhiel
41 b.   © Photo: Nacása &
        Partners inc.
43–45   © Photo: Mitsumasa
        Fujitsuka
46/47   © Photo: Tomio Ohashi
48 t.   © Photo: Toshiharu
        Kitajima
48 b.   © Fumihiko Maki
49   © Toshiharu Kitajima
51   © Photo: Friedrich
        Busam/Architekturphoto
52   © Photo: Kazumi Kurigami
54   © Photo: Shinkenchiku-sha
55   © Photo: Dennis Gilbert/
        Arcaid
56/57   © Photo: Arnaud
        Carpentier
58   © Photo: Richard Bryant
        1993/Arcaid
59   © Photo: David Churchill
        1993/Arcaid
60   © Photo: Jörg Hempel/
        Architekton
61 t.   © Santiago Calatrava
61 b.   © Photo: Jörg Hempel/
        Architekton
62   © Photo: Richard Bryant
        1992/Arcaid

63   © Arquitectonica
64/65   © Photo: Antonio Martinelli
66   © Photo: Cesar Pelli &
        Associates/Renderer:
        Lee Dunnette
67   © Photo: K.L.Ng/Aga
        KhanTrust for Culture
68/69   © Photo: John Back
70   © Photo: Jim Steinkamp
71–73   © Photo: Paul Warchol
72 t.   © Steven Holl
74/75   © Photo: Grant Mudford
75 b.   © Hodgetts and Fung
76/77   © Photo: Friedrich Busam/
        Architekturphoto
78/79   © Photo: Dieter
        Leistner/Architekton
81   © Joshua White
82   © Photo: Jacqueline
        Guillot
84–87   © Photo: Alfred Wolf
88 t.   © Photo: Christian Richters
88 b.   © Photo: Joshua White
89 t.   © Photo: Ralph Richter/
        Architekturphoto
89 b.   © Frank O. Gehry &
        Associates, Inc.
90/91   © Photo: Dieter Leistner/
        Architekton
92   © Photo: Hayes Davidson/
        Richard Davies
93/94   © Photo: Alfred Wolf
95–97   © Photo: Katsuaki Furudate
98–101 © Photo: Arnaud
        Carpentier
102 t. © Photo: Grant Mudford
102 b. © Franklin Israel
103   © Photo: Grant Mudford
104/105 © Photo: Timothy Hursley
106 t. © Antoine Predock
106/107 © Photo: Timothy Hursley
109   © Photo: Antonio
        Martinelli
110   © Massimiliano Fuksas
112   © Photo: Y. Futagawa/Vitra
113   © Photo: Richard Bryant/
        Vitra
114   © Photo: Shinkenchiku-sha
115 t. © Photo: Arnaud
        Carpentier
115 b. © Fumihiko Maki
116   © Photo: Arnaud
        Carpentier
117   © Photo: Toshiharu
        Kitajima
118/119 © Photo: Scott Frances/
        Esto
119 b. © Richard Meier
120/121 © Photo: Arnaud
        Carpentier
122   © Christian de Portzamparc

123   © Photo: Alfred Wolf
124/125 © Photo: Timothy Hursley
126   © Massimiliano Fuksas
127   © Photo: Antonio
        Martinelli
129–134 © Photo: Arnaud
        Carpentier
135 t. © Photo: Roy Wright
        Photography Inc.
135 c. © Photo: Masashi Kudo
137   © Christian de Portzamparc
138/139 © Photo: Arnaud
        Carpentier
140/141 © Photo: Philippe Ruault
143   © VG Bild-Kunst, Bonn,
        1996
144   © Christo 1995/Photo:
        Wolfgang Volz
146/147 © Christo 1995/Photo:
        Wolfgang Volz
148/149 © Photo: Dieter
        Leistner/Architekton
150   © Photo: Hisao
        Suzuki/Archivo Eye
151 t. © Photo: Aki Furudate
151 b. © Massimiliano Fuksas
152   © VG Bild-Kunst, Bonn
        1996/© Documentation
        du Musée Nationale d'Art
        Moderne – Centre
        Georges Pompidou – Paris,
        Photo: Adam Rzepka
153   © VG Bild-Kunst, Bonn
        1996/© Photo: Rheini-
        sches Bildarchiv Köln
154   © Photo: Roger Guillemot
155   © VG Bild-Kunst, Bonn
        1996/©Photo: Roger
        Guillemot
157   © Photo: Alfred Wolf
159/160 © Photo: Arnaud
        Carpentier
161   © Photo: Bill
        Jacobson/DIA
162   © Photo: Arnaud
        Carpentier
163   © David Hockney,
        1995/Photo: Steve Oliver
164   © Photo: 1994 Norman
        McGrath
165   © Photo: Jeff
        Goldberg/Esto
166 t. © Photo: Timothy Hursley
166 b. © Josh Schweitzer
167   © Photo: Timothy Hursley
168/169 © VG Bild-Kunst, Bonn,
        1996
170/171 © Photo: Eduard
        Hueber/Arch Photo
171 b. © Simon Ungers
172   © Lebbeus Woods

173   © Photo: 1992 Norman
        McGrath
174   © Photo: Alfred Wolf
175 l. © Photo: Alfred Wolf
175 r. © VG Bild-Kunst, Bonn
        1996/© Photo: Alfred
        Wolf
176   © Shin Takamatsu
177   © Photo: Arnaud
        Carpentier
179   © Photo: Alfred Wolf
180   © Photo: Paul Warchol
182 t. © Tadao Ando
182/183 © Photo: Alfred Wolf
184   © Photo: Taisuke Ogawa
185 t. © Photo: Itsuko Hasegawa
185 b. © Photo: Taisuke Ogawa
186/187 © Photo: Arnaud
        Carpentier
188/189 © Photo: ARTOG/
        D.G. Olshavsky
190/191 © Photo: Richard
        Bryant/Vitra
192   © Photo: Alfred Wolf
193   © Photo: Arnaud
        Carpentier
194   © Photo: Paul Warchol
195   © Photo: 1995 Norman
        McGrath
196 t. © Photo: Arnaud Carpentier
196 b. © Wes Jones
197 l. © Photo: Erich Koyama
197 r. © Photo: Arnaud
        Carpentier
198/199 © Photo: Paul H. Groh
200   © Photo: Todd
        Conversano
201   © Photo: Tom Bonner
202 t. © Bart Prince
202/203 © Photo: Michele M.
        Penhall
204   © Nuclear Electric
205–207 © SITE
209   © Richard Davies
210/211 © Photo: Christian
        Richters
212   © Photo: Hisao Suzuki/
        Archivo Eye
213–215 © Photo: Paul Raftery/
        Arcaid
216   © Photo: J. C. Planchet
217   © Photo: Alfred Wolf
218/219 © Photo: Richard
        Bryant/Vitra
220/221 © Photo: Reinhard
        Görner/Architektur-
        fotografie
222–225 © Photo: Valode & Pistre

The publisher and author wish to
thank each of the architects and
photographers for their assistance.

Dietrich Wildung

Henri Stierlin

Hasan-Uddin Khan

egypt
From Prehistory to the Romans

greece
From Mycenae to the Parthenon

international style
Modernist Architecture from 1925 to 1965

TASCHEN

TASCHEN

TASCHEN

Egypt
From Prehistory to the Romans
Dietrich Wildung
240 pp., c. 300 colour ills.
Softcover

Greece
From Mycenae to the Parthenon
Henri Stierlin
240 pp., c. 300 colour ills.
Softcover

International Style
Modernist Architecture from 1925 to 1965
Hasan–Uddin Khan
240 pp., c. 300 colour ills.
Softcover

Henri Stierlin

Philip Jodidio

Xavier Barral i Altet

the maya
Palaces and pyramids of the rainforest

new forms
Architecture in the 1990s

the romanesque
Towns, Cathedrals and Monasteries

TASCHEN

TASCHEN

TASCHEN

The Maya
Palaces and pyramids of the rainforest
Henri Stierlin
240 pp., c. 300 colour ills.
Softcover

New Forms
Architecture in the 1990s
Philip Jodidio
240 pp., c. 300 colour ills.
Softcover

The Romanesque
Towns, Cathedrals and Monasteries
Xavier Barral i Altet
240 pp., c. 300 colour ills.
Softcover

"An excellently produced, informative guide to the history of architecture. Accessible to everyone."
Architektur Aktuell, Vienna

"This is by far the most comprehensive review of recent years."
Frankfurter Rundschau, Frankfurt

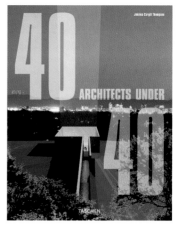

"A landmark guide to the latest innovations in space, light and form."
Perspective, UK

Architecture Now!
Philip Jodidio
576 pp., c. 570 ills.
Flexi-cover

Modernism Rediscovered
Pierluigi Serraino
Julius Shulman
576 pp., 840 ills.
Flexi-cover

40 architects under 40
Jessica Cargill Thompson
560 pp., 550 ills.
Flexi-cover